THE MAJESTIC TAPESTRY

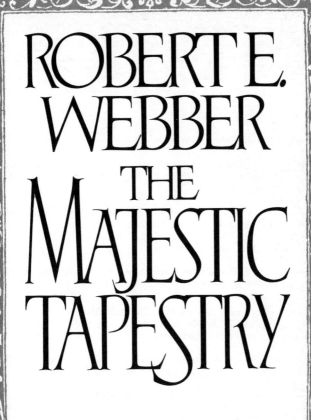

ROBERT E. WEBBER

THE MAJESTIC TAPESTRY

THOMAS NELSON PUBLISHERS
Nashville • Camden • New York

Published in Nashville, Tennessee, by Thomas Nelson, Inc., and distributed in Canada by Lawson Falle, Ltd., Cambridge, Ontario.

Printed in the United States of America.

Unless otherwise noted, the Bible version used in this publication is THE NEW KING JAMES VERSION. Copyright © 1979, 1980, 1982, Thomas Nelson, Inc., Publishers.

Scripture quotations noted NIV are from The Holy Bible: New International Version. Copyright © 1973, 1978, International Bible Society. Used by permission of Zondervan Bible Publishers.

Scripture quotations noted LB are from *The Living Bible* (Wheaton, Ill.: Tyndale House Publishers, 1971) and are used by permission.

Scripture quotations noted RSV are from the Revised Standard Version of the Bible, copyrighted 1946, 1952, © 1971, 1973 by the Division of Christian Education of the National Council of Churches in the U.S.A. and used by permission.

Library of Congress Cataloging-in-Publication Data

Webber, Robert.
  The majestic tapestry.

  Bibliography: p. 231
  1. Theology—Early church, ca. 30–600.   2. Christian life—Early church, ca. 30–600.   3. Evangelicalism.
I. Title.
BT25.W43   1986   270.1   86–16415
ISBN 0-8407-5536-8

Contents

Preface

In the spring of 1977 a group of forty evangelical theologians and leaders gathered outside of Chicago to hammer out the Chicago Call. The essence of this Call urged evangelical churches to turn away from an ahistorical Christianity to recover new, enriching insights from the early church.

In the succeeding years this return to an interest in the early church exceeded the expectations of those of us who drafted the Chicago Call. However, we would all recognize that the renewed interest was not because of the Chicago Call. Rather, the Call was simply an expression of what was already happening in the Catholic church, many mainline Protestant churches, many charismatic churches, and among a number of evangelicals.

In 1978 my book *Common Roots: A Call to Evangelical Maturity* urged a return to the traditions of the early church. This book, *The Majestic Tapestry,* is a rewrite and update of *Common Roots*.

The principal difference is found in the fact that much

that I called for in 1978 has happened. Therefore, I have rewritten the book in such a way that it no longer constitutes a call to evangelical maturity, as the old subtitle indicated, but now describes how the early Christian tradition can enrich contemporary faith as stated in the new subtitle.

A second major difference in this updated edition is in the recognition that the work of Christ is the thread that ties all the aspects of the Christian tradition together. In 1978 when *Common Roots* was written, I didn't grasp the *integrating principle* of the work of Christ in the same sense that I do today. The new title for my book, *The Majestic Tapestry,* reflects this deeper understanding.

I wish to express particular thanks to my editors, Michael Hyatt, Etta Wilson, and Stephen Hines. Michael encouraged me to rewrite *Common Roots* and to arrange for its republication through Thomas Nelson. Etta wisely sent me back to the drawing board when I left too much of the original *Common Roots* out of the rewrite. And she urged me to personalize it; I hope that personal element now comes through. Thanks also to Stephen Hines for his helpful attention to detail.

Finally, I wish to express an enormous thanks to my typist Mary Lou McCurdy. She has put in a number of extra hours as this manuscript was typed and retyped. To all these people and to others, my students and my family, who put up with my absence and intense periods of concentration, I owe a special debt of gratitude.

*The dear Fathers wished, by their writings,
to lead us to the Scriptures.*

MARTIN LUTHER

INTRODUCTION

1
THE RETURN TO TRADITION

Evangelicals are becoming engaged in a heated discussion about the significance of early Christian tradition. Some argue that it is irrelevant for today's church and not worthy of discussion. Some feel neutral toward the church Fathers. Others are arguing that early church tradition is a source for a significant renewal and enrichment of our personal and corporate spiritual life.

The discussion reminds me somewhat of the debate that surrounded *Fiddler on the Roof* when it was in its early stages of development. As the creators of that great musical worked on it, they discovered it was about the paradox of tradition in a society where old values were disintegrating. It was then that the choreographer, Jerome Robbins, concluded, "Well, if it's a show about tradition and its dissolution, then the audience should be told what the tradition is."[1]

I sense that the situation in the church today is somewhat similar to the tension described in *Fiddler on the Roof*. Many people feel that we live in a culture where old values have been lost. *Even the church has lost its tradition*. Consequently, the church "should be told what the tradition is."

So, my purpose in writing this book, like *Fiddler on the Roof,* is to tell the Christian tradition. I believe that if we are going to debate the pros and cons of early Christian tradition for today, we ought at least to know what we agree or disagree with and how it may help us or hurt us. My conviction is that the early tradition of the church will do more than help us. It will renew our faith and fill us with a new sense of joy. It will revitalize our churches and fill them with new zest and power!

WHAT IS THE CHRISTIAN TRADITION?

Those who object to the current interest in the tradition of the early church do so because they fear a study of the early church will lead them into the Roman Catholic church. While there have been several notable cases of evangelicals' becoming Roman Catholics (Thomas Howard, Sheldon Vanauken, Malcolm Muggeridge), the trend is clearly not in that direction. The early church was not Roman Catholic. Instead, it represented the common tradition of the whole church, a tradition that belongs to Protestants as much as it belongs to Catholic and to Orthodox Christians. This point can be clearly understood when we make a distinction between the tradition of the church and later traditions developed by Orthodox, Catholic, or Protestant Christians.

In this book I will refer to tradition as *the broad outline of Christian belief and practice developed from the Scriptures between the time of Christ and the middle of the fifth century.* This has been called "the classical Christian tradition."

In the following chapters I will summarize the relevant aspects of the classical tradition that were developed in the early church—especially those convictions regarding Christ, the church, worship, spirituality, the mission of the church, and authority. I want to deal with the basic Christian threads of the Christian tapestry, threads that I have happily discovered to be intrinsically interwoven into a majestic work of thought and experience. And I want to show you how those threads can enrich and are enriching contemporary faith.

I regard traditions (in the plural) as something other than tradition. Traditions are additional layers of thought that have been placed upon the original tradition. They are the convictions that divide Catholic, mainline Protestant, and evangelical churches.

For example, in the theology of salvation one church may emphasize free will, another may stress election, and another may attempt to combine the two. However, it is the common tradition of salvation in Christ that lies behind these various traditions. What I want to do, then, is to identify the common tradition that lies behind our traditions. Our *common tradition* is more important than the *traditions* that divide us. And I think the common tradition has the power to change our lives and our churches.

WHO IS BEING DRAWN TO THE CHRISTIAN TRADITION?

The people being drawn to the tradition—either instinctively or through study of the early church—are the people of various renewing movements. They are in the process of rediscovering the primary truths of the Christian faith. Specifically, these groups include: (1) Catholic churches affected by the various awakenings such as RENEW and Cursillo, a movement that has spread to mainline Protestant churches as well, and (2) mainline Protestant churches affected by denominational renewal movements. Renewal, for example, is taking place in all the mainline churches—Methodist, Presbyterian, Baptist, and Congregationalist, to name a few; (3) but there is also the emergence of a new evangelical movement that has grown out of the Jesus movement of the sixties and that includes such groups as Samaritan's Purse, Youth with a Mission, Last Days Ministries, Sojourners, Calvary Chapels, Vineyards, and hundreds of independent Christian fellowships centering around worship and the practical application of biblical teaching. Finally, (4) the many charismatic movements that have swept through nearly every denomination and have affected the church worldwide constitute a group discovering its connection to the early church.

Throughout this work I will refer to these movements and others like them as the *renewing church*. I have not attempted to provide a statistical study of this group. Nevertheless, I believe the comments I will make about them are generally true. This book will be of help to these renewing movements because *it will name what they have instinctively experienced—the power of the early Christian tradition*.

I believe the return to Christian tradition is a work of God in our time. From the divine point of view the Holy Spirit seems to be working a new thing in the church, particularly among the members of the younger generation. For example, the headlines of a recent issue of the *New York Times* read "Spiritual Life Returning to Campuses." The heart of the article dealt with the experience of college chaplains who had observed "a deeper commitment of faith along with a *keener appreciation of tradition among students*" (italics mine).

I believe the emerging interest in the Christian tradition is connected to the American phenomenon of the baby-boomer generation, that generation of 75.9 million people born between 1946 and 1964. In 1986 the oldest of this group turn forty and the youngest turn twenty-two. The twenty-two-year-olds are graduating from college and starting careers, whereas the forty-year-olds have begun to take leadership positions in government, business, education, and the church.

This new generation of Christians differs significantly from the older generation of Christians. On religious issues the older generation is attracted to the details of theological systems, tends to think in exclusive either/or terms, enjoys debates over theological points, tends to be passive regarding social issues, and wants to maintain things as they are. They have been shaped by the values of a society recovering from the depression and World War II. Therefore, they opt for security and stability over change. But the newer generation has been shaped by the values of a country reeling from the revolution of the sixties and shaped by technology and the communications revolution of sight, sound, and action. Consequently, the new generation is geared toward change and dynamic development.

Although the above characterizations of the older and newer generations are not true of everyone, they do stand as generalizations. Let me give you an example. Recently, my wife and I were having dinner with her father, a man recognized as an evangelical statesman. As we were bantering religious issues back and forth he said, "Why don't you write something that speaks to the great issues of the day?" "What, for example?" I asked. "Why don't you write on the inspiration of the Bible or address the issue of Christianity and communism?" he questioned. My wife, always ready to come to my defense, said, "But Dad, that's your issue . . . Bob's generation isn't interested in those issues . . . they are interested in worship, spirituality, social action."

She had made the point and made it well. The difference between the older generation of evangelical leaders and the newer generation is captured in the issues. The younger generation has a different agenda. It is back to the basics, back to the tradition. The older generation seems to be interested in what divides Christians—perhaps as a way of maintaining distinctives. The younger generation seems interested in what unites Christians—perhaps as a way of affirming the unity they have experienced with other Christians at inter-church conferences where they have shared increased dialogue and social agenda contacts.

In an attempt to describe the Christian leadership that will be provided by this new generation, Chuck Smith, the pastor of Calvary Chapel of Dana Point, California, a congregation of baby boomers, wrote an article entitled "Where Are They Taking Us?"[2] He argued that baby-boomer Christians are new consensus thinkers who are willing to draw on a variety of Christian traditions. They are no longer locked into old theological views that are positioned against other viewpoints. Rather, he said: "These believers are remaining faithful to the basic tenets of Christianity. At the same time, they are very willing to investigate the perspective of fellow believers from the other side of the fence. They are suspicious of religious institutions that try to force people into mental stockades. Very few of them accept church doctrines or norms simply because 'the pastor says so.' "

Smith then suggested five characteristics of baby-boomer Christians: (1) They have a biblically informed and expanded world-view; (2) they stress both relational and doctrinal commitment; (3) they believe theology is dynamic not static; (4) they stress the importance of encountering God through worship; and (5) they distinguish between non-negotiable doctrines and negotiable practices.

Chuck Smith certainly has described me and many people I know. The kind of Christianity that attracts me is one that emphasizes primary truths. I'm more interested in broad strokes than detail, more attracted to an inclusive view of the faith than an exclusive view, more concerned with unity than diversity, more open to a dynamic growing faith than to a static fixed system, more concerned with relationships than with doctrines; and I am more visual than verbal and have a high level of tolerance for ambiguity.

It is here at these points that the link between the ancient tradition and the new generation can be made. The early tradition of the faith dealt with basic issues, was inclusive, concerned with unity, open and dynamic, mystical, relational, visual, and tangible. For this reason, when I became exposed to the tradition of the early church, I readily embraced it.

WHY TELL THE CHRISTIAN TRADITION AGAIN?

I am convinced that the primary reason to tell the Christian tradition is because of its power to renew faith. Early Christian teaching is simple and uncluttered by the addition of later layers of tradition. It cuts through the complexities of culturized Christianity and allows what is primary and essential to surface.

The Christian tradition is sorely needed in the Christian church because many people like myself have come to the end of our patience with so-called innovative gimmicks that have no connection with the past. We are exhausted by every new trick in the book, so now we are digging into the past to resurrect old treasures that still have meaning and can offer direction.

Of course, retelling the Christian tradition also accents what is common in the faith. Frankly, I view divisiveness between churches based on differences in secondary theological issues as intolerable. What is truly important are those truths the church universal holds in common. My own search for the unity that exists between believing Catholic, Orthodox, Protestant, evangelical, and charismatic Christians has taken me back to the common era and to those roots that belong to the whole church. These are convictions that *precede* a time when the church became *Eastern* Orthodox, *Roman* Catholic, or *Protestant*.

Finally, I have found that telling the Christian tradition again links the past with the future. The old adage that those who would shape the future must know the past still stands. If we would shape the future of the church in continuity with its past, we need to know its tradition and why it has endured for so long.

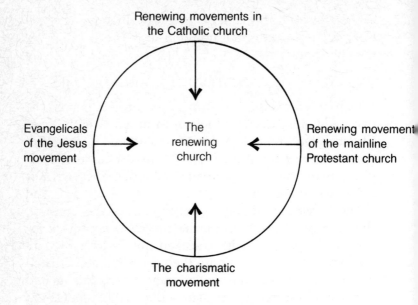

WHY HAS THIS BOOK BEEN WRITTEN AND FOR WHOM?

I have written *The Majestic Tapestry* primarily for the people who find themselves on a spiritual journey, the people of the renewing church. But it will be of interest to Christian people outside the renewing church, for it will provide insights into what is happening in the church today.

This book can benefit the people of the renewing church in several ways. First, it may be read as *a primer on the Christian faith*. I intend to spell out in a clear fashion the most essential truths of traditional Christianity and suggest ways these truths can enrich the contemporary church.

Unfortunately, we often deal with specific aspects of the Christian faith in isolation from the whole. We seldom look beyond specific threads to see the whole tapestry. We get caught up in the details of the tapestry, dwelling on this or that thread or color. Consequently, we fail to see the interwovenness of the absolute essentials, those main threads that bind the tapestry together and create the pattern.

As a primer this book looks at the basic threads, the threads that we deal with in our everyday experience of the Christian life. And since these are the basic threads of the faith, they are the common threads, the ones that unite all Christians. Therefore, the book has value for Catholics, Protestants, evangelicals, charismatics, and others to remind them of their shared heritage.

Second, I think this book provides an *explanation of what is happening in the church today*. There are many people involved in the renewing churches today who have not been given an interpretation of their personal and corporate experience. This, of course, is not unusual. Frequently, when we are in the midst of change, we may know that things are changing, but we may not understand where the change is taking us. By reading this book people who are involved in the renewing church will understand what is happening not only in their local church, but in the renewing church throughout the world. They will have a better idea of where the renewing church is headed.

Finally, the book may be read as *a self-portrait*. I didn't grasp this dimension of the work until a friend of mine in his midthirties read the manuscript. As he was reading, he exclaimed, "Why this is like a self-portrait . . . I see myself and my experience everywhere!" This person, a member of the baby-boomer generation, felt the book identified what he had experienced but was not yet able to articulate.

Throughout history a revived interest in the insights of the early church has usually been accompanied by signifi-

The Majestic Tapestry

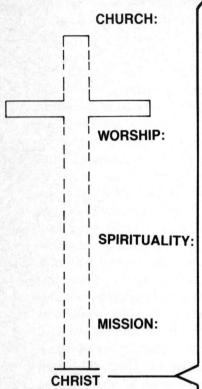

CHURCH:

<u>The primary extension of Christ in the world</u>
The community of God's people through whom the work of Christ is extended to the world is the church, the sign of redemption.

WORSHIP:

<u>The primary celebration of the church</u>
In worship the church proclaims and acts out Christ and his redeeming work, making it present in all its power among God's people.

SPIRITUALITY:

<u>The primary life of the church</u>
Spirituality is a participation in Christ, a personal sharing in the victory of Christ over the power of evil.

MISSION:

<u>The primary work of the church</u>
The church extends the benefits of Christ's life, death, and resurrection to the world through evangelism, education, and social action.

CHRIST
In Christ the powers of evil are defeated and the world is restored.

AUTHORITY:

<u>The primary document of the church</u>
The church's vision and work in the world is authoritatively set forth in the apostolic tradition, the Scriptures. These truths are summarized in the church's creed and reflected on in the ongoing task of theology.

cant renewal in the church. For example, both Luther and Calvin drew heavily on the early church Fathers. Then, in the seventeenth century, when the fires of the Reformation were burning low, Philip Jacob Spener, the leader of the Pietist movement in Germany, called upon the people to recover the kind of Christianity taught and practiced by the early Christians. After citing Tertullian, Ignatius, Eusebius, Justin and others, Spener wrote: "It [the early church] demonstrates that what we are seeking is not impossible . . . it is the same Holy Spirit who is bestowed on us by God, who once effected all things in the early Christian, and he is neither less able nor less active today to accomplish the work of sanctification in us."[3]

If Luther, Calvin, and Spener could speak to us today, they would assure us that the tapestry of the early Christian tradition is simple and compelling. They would call on us to restore the main threads, to let what is central to the faith shine forth in bold relief. That is already being done in the renewing church; the pattern that is emerging is a thing of beauty.

I hope you will read this book with the sense that it can do something for you. You may sense that you are on a spiritual journey; you know that you cannot remain where you are; you know that something is happening inside you. You may not be able to put your finger on it, but you know that some very deep changes are occurring in your spiritual outlook. This book will help you to understand yourself and will point you in directions that will be helpful.

*So the Lord now manifestly came to his
own, and, born by his own created
order which he himself bears, he
by his obedience on the tree renewed
and reversed what was done by disobedience
in connection with a tree.*

IRENAEUS, A.D. 180

SECTION I

*The Tradition about the Work
of Christ*

The Tradition about the Work of Christ

When I was a child, I loved to put together puzzles. Whenever I became sick with a cold or the flu, my mother would ask, "What do you want to entertain yourself with until you are well enough to go back to school?" I always said, "Get me a puzzle—the bigger the better."

I loved missing school and enjoyed even more the opportunity to have a full day to work on the puzzle. My mother would spread the puzzle out on a large card table placed by my bed, and I would enthusiastically set myself to an analysis of it before making any attempt to put it together. My first concern was always to find the key, the central image around which all the other parts of the puzzle fitted. And when I found the key, the rest of the puzzle seemed to fall quickly into place around it.

I have found that whether I'm dealing with a puzzle, a tapestry, or the Christian faith, the complexity of it is gathered around a central piece, a dominant thread, a basic conviction. In the Christian faith the piece of the puzzle, or the dominant thread, is the work of Jesus Christ. Once we have a solid grasp of the meaning of his work, the rest of the faith falls together around it.

As far back as I can remember, I was told that the work of Christ was central to the Christian faith. However, several years ago when I began to reflect on the teaching I had received, I realized that the importance of the death of Christ was always explained in terms of my personal salvation, little more. I was told that Christ had paid the price for my sin so that by faith in his death I could be a forgiven sinner. I do not reject that teaching.

Nevertheless, I have come to see through the study of the early Christian tradition that my view of the work of Christ was severely limited. It wasn't that I didn't believe the right truth. I simply didn't understand how far-reaching and all-inclusive the work of Christ really was. When I discovered the universal and cosmic nature of the work of Christ, it was like being born again, again. I was given the key to a Christian way of viewing the whole world, a key that unlocked the door to a rich storehouse of spiritual treasures, treasures that I am still handling in sheer amazement.

What I have discovered among these treasures is a tapestry of historical events, all of which are related to the main event of human history—the living, dying, and rising again of Jesus Christ.

The specific historical threads of this tapestry are the creation, the fall, the call of Israel, the incarnation, the death, resurrection, and ascension of Christ, the experience of Pentecost, the birth of the church, the coming again of Christ, the consummation of history, and the creation of a new heaven and a new earth. These historical events tell a story that sweeps from the beginning of time to the end.

For me these are the most important events of human history. They link heaven and earth, God and man, immaterial and material, eternity and time. They give meaning to my life and constitute the story out of which I live as a Christian (see Col. 1:15–23).

The Fathers of the early church put the pieces of this story into a grand tapestry. For them the elements of the story are all interrelated. One thread does not exist without the other. The key thread, the one that reaches out to tie all the others together, the one that runs through the center of it all, is the work of Christ. I want to explain that work more fully and show how the early church's understanding of that work can enrich our faith today.

2
THE WORK OF CHRIST IN THE EARLY CHURCH

CHRIST IS VICTOR

The early church was convinced that the work of Christ was a great victory over sin, the devil, and the domain of darkness. The best description of the victory of Christ over the power of evil is found in Irenaeus, the second century defender of the faith.

When I first came across Irenaeus's interpretation, I was struggling with what I considered to be a very limited view of Christ's death. I saw myself as a sinner and in need of salvation. I had trusted in Christ as the one who made things right with the Father for *me*. But I had no sense of how the death of Christ was for the whole world. Irenaeus took me by the hand and led me into that new understanding, an understanding that was to enrich my whole view of the Christian faith.

I discovered that I had an individualistic understanding of the work of Christ. I had taken the rugged individualism common to us Americans and read my Bible through that grid. Consequently, I saw the work of Christ as applying to me and to this or that person but not to the whole world.

The first thing that Irenaeus did for me was to help me discover the biblical teaching that sin is not only individual but also extends to everything in the world; everything including relationships, nature, and institutions such as the family, the state, and economic systems have been affected by sin. I began to sense, as Paul said, that "the creation was subjected to futility," that the creation was under a "bondage of corruption" (Rom. 8:20–21).

Second, Irenaeus helped me to see the biblical teaching that the work of Christ defeated evil and its power in the world. What I began to understand was the Pauline teaching that "the creation itself also will be delivered from the bondage" (Rom. 8:21).

In no way did this decrease my sense of personal salvation. Instead, it took me beyond the reduction I had made of Christ's work and led me into the sense of how far-reaching and extensive the work of Christ really is. Although I had been grateful for my own salvation, this new sense of the cosmic salvation which Christ brings to his whole creation lifted my spirit into new bursts of praise to the Father. In the early church this overwhelming theme of a salvation for the whole creation was called the *theology of recapitulation*. Let me explain recapitulation in more detail.

RECAPITULATION

When Paul wrote to the Ephesians he spoke of the recapitulation of all things in Christ. The word *recapitulation* appears in the middle of a long sentence that begins at Ephesians 1:7 and ends with verse 12:

> Having made known to us the mystery of His will, according to His good pleasure which He purposed in Himself, that in the dispensation of the fullness of the times He might *gather together* [recapitulate] in one all things in Christ, both which are in heaven and which are on earth (Eph. 1:9–12, italics mine).

To the early church the theme of the recapitulation of all things because of the victory of Christ over Satan was seen as the fundamental result of Christ's death. It was the thread into which everything else was gathered, for it reached out into every piece of the tapestry and put the entire Christian vision of reality into focus.

Irenaeus summarized the Pauline theme of the recapitulation this way:

> So the Lord now manifestly came to his own, and born by his own created order which he himself bears, he by his obedience on the tree renewed and reversed what was done by disobedience in connection with a tree; . . . He therefore completely renewed all things.[1]

Irenaeus showed how the work of Christ was understood in terms of the salvation of the entire creation. God not only saved persons, but through the work of Christ, the restoration, renewal, and the re-creation of the entire universe was foreshadowed. This overarching view of history built on the vision of Isaiah (65:17–25) and Paul (Rom. 8:20–24).

As I studied the theme of recapitulation more deeply, I discovered that the extensive nature of Christ's work was expressed through three motifs set forth by Irenaeus. First, I realized that the focal point of everything in the Christian faith and all of life is the incarnation, death, and resurrection. Second, I began to understand how the incarnation, death, and resurrection reach back to the Creation and the Fall to help me grasp the limitation of evil in the world. Third, the Fathers showed me how the incarnation, death, and resurrection reach into the future restoration of creation, and how I can have hope in the midst of evil. The Fathers taught me how the entire universe and all of history, from the creation of the world to the new heaven and earth, are gathered into Christ.

Let me expand on these three themes to show how comprehensive the work of Christ really is and how worthy God is of our praise and service.

CHRISTUS VICTOR AS THE FOCAL POINT

First, I discovered that the center of the Christian vision of the world is the death and resurrection of Christ. In my individualistic view of the death of Christ I believed Christ died to pay the penalty for the sins of individuals only. I believed that Jesus satisfied the justice of God through his death. I believed that God became free to be merciful to me through the death of his Son. God was therefore just and the justifier of the unjust (Rom. 8:21–26). Now I believe that the biblical basis of that teaching should never be denied, yet I am also convinced that it is not all that the Scriptures teach about the death of Jesus.

The early church Fathers emphasized the biblical teaching that Christ *by his satisfaction for sin attained a victory over the devil and the kingdom of evil*. The result of this victory is that Christ assures the restoration of all things to their original condition and beyond—*Christus Victor*. This is the theme that is the key to a dynamic vision of life held by early Christians . . . a theme being recovered today in the renewing church. Allow me to explain this biblical idea a little further before I comment on how it has renewed my faith.

Irenaeus explained the relationship between the Incarnation and the death of Christ in a moving way. He captured that relationship in this phrase: "born by his own created order which he himself bears." Let me explain this statement with a common illustration. (My illustration does not capture the full meaning of what I want to communicate, but it is a place to start.) Imagine that you have built a beautiful sand castle on the beach. Then, after completing this work of creation, you stand back to admire it.

All of a sudden a large wave comes and destroys it, and you stand back, sadly watching your work collapse. If your instinct is like mine, you will probably want to build it over again.

Now apply this simple illustration to the idea of recapitulation. God's sand castle is the world. The wave is the power of the evil one. In my illustration God chooses to rebuild the world, to restore it, to re-create it. But he chooses to do this act of re-creation, not from the outside as he did in the beginning, but from the inside (my analogy breaks down a bit at this point, as analogies do). This is recapitulation . . . doing it over again. God rebuilds his creation.

With this illustration in mind, let me use some biblical and early church language in a story that will relate *Christus Victor* to the recapitulation, the creating over again of the universe.

When God created the universe, he looked at his created order and declared that it was good. He was pleased with what he brought into existence out of nothing, for it was the product of his own creativity. He had created time, space, sound, color, shape, life, animals, humankind—all things. The sight of it gave him great pleasure. However, as a result of the power of the evil one, the harmony and beauty of his work of creation had been spoiled. Now hate, greed, chaos, and disharmony raged in his creation. And although creation itself remained good, the power of evil working through people and the institutions of society such as government and the economic order brought the pain and misery of dehumanization into the creation.

God could have destroyed the creation and started over. Instead he chose to *become* his creation and re-create the creation from the inside by destroying the power of death and sin that ravaged it. This is the meaning of the phrase, "born by his own created order which he himself bears."

In the Incarnation the Creator *became* the creation and took upon himself the distortion of sin that extended not only into people but also into every corner of nature and every institution of society. By his death he, the Creator, destroyed the power of death and sin. And by his resurrection, he, the Creator, demonstrated the power to re-create. Consequently, by virtue of the incarnation, death, and resurrection, Christ has triumphed over the power of sin in his creation. And at his second coming he will completely destroy the power of sin over his creation, releasing it from the "bondage to decay" it is now under.

In this view the Fathers taught that Christ not only died to satisfy the requirements of justice but also taught that he gained a victory over the powers of evil that raged in his world. His work on the cross, which extends to all of life, is the downfall of the powers of evil. The havoc they have wrought in the entire created order cannot and will not prevail, for his victory over them is the promise of the ultimate restoration of his creation. This view helps me to understand that evil is not the final word of God's universe.

CHRISTUS VICTOR AND THE FALL

Irenaeus captured the biblical view of the relationship between the work of Christ and evil in these words: "He therefore completely renewed all things, both taking up the battle against our enemy, and crushing him who at the beginning had led us captive in Adam." The emphasis on the renewal of all things recognized the disorder that permeates every aspect of creation.

Irenaeus and other early church Fathers understood evil in terms of the "powers." For them sin was not merely doing bad deeds. Rather, it was a rebellion against the authority of God—a rebellion that expressed itself when Adam and Eve and their posterity chose to put themselves under the power of the evil one.

What the Fathers led me to was the biblical idea that when Adam and Eve fell, the demonic powers of evil were unleashed against the created order. Paul related that these powers "in which you once walked according to the course of this world" are the powers of evil which are at work in the creation (Eph. 2:2). Like the wave that destroys the sand castle, the powers of evil distort and pervert God's good creation. They make social institutions become evil things, terrorizing people, plundering the environment, aborting babies, threatening nuclear holocaust. The powers of evil rob the earth of its joy and turn history into madness.

The Fathers of the church understood the biblical teaching that the work of Jesus Christ triumphed over these powers. Christ's work not only stops the waves from destroying the castle but begins the work of reconstruction. Irenaeus, speaking of God's work through Christ, said, "He therefore completely renewed all things."

I believe that the sin of Adam brought sin, death, and condemnation to the entire universe. But I believe that Christ, the Second Adam, broke the power of sin by his obedience to the Father and through his incarnation, death, and resurrection effected a restoration of the primal condition of creation. Christ reversed the effects of the Fall and brought righteousness, life, and justification to the entire creation.

With the early church I believe that sin is conquered, and the creation is set free. What the Fathers developed was the Pauline theme that "the creation itself also will be delivered from the bondage of corruption into the glorious liberty of the children of God" (Rom. 8:21). I now see how the Christian teaching about creation and the Fall are intrinsically linked with the work of Christ. Creation and the Fall are not intellectual objects of inquiry. Rather, they are part of the story of existence, parts of the story that can only be truly understood in the light of *Christus Victor*. Through Christ the powers of evil have suffered an irreversible defeat! With the early church I confess that with my whole heart.

CHRISTUS VICTOR AND THE RESTORATION OF THE WORLD

The work of Christ not only helps me understand how evil is defeated but it also is the source of my understanding of future events. I used to think of the future in terms of a series of events that were to happen before the coming of Jesus. I took great delight in debating such things as the Rapture, the Tribulation, the Millennium and the Judgment. The important thing was to determine *when* the end-times events were going to happen, as well as the why and the how of them.

But *Christus Victor* has shifted my attention away from the events surrounding the end times. I no longer try to project when these things might happen. Instead, my attention is now on the meaning of the coming of Christ for the world. I seek to live in the hope of the full recapitulation of all things. Rather than holding to an intellectual view about the coming of Christ, I now hold his coming in my heart where it shapes my interpretation of the events in my life as well as the events of history.

Christ's work of recapitulation is the key to the future. With the early church we believe Christ has rooted out the enemy. He has destroyed the power of sin and death in his own death. He has demonstrated the renewal of all things by his resurrection. Christ, we proclaim, will rule over a restored universe. This is no mere creedal statement, but a living hope which we celebrate in worship and experience in our lives.

This hope, the expectation of the renewal of all things in Christ, is also the vision in which the whole church lives. No matter how effectively the powers of evil now rage, they are doomed. Evil is not ultimate. Evil is not the last word in human existence. The last word is Jesus Christ. The vision of a new heaven and a new earth in Isaiah (65:17–23) and John (Rev. 20–22) is no fantasy. It is the reality, the truth. Therefore, it is the hope that lies behind everything we do as Christians.

Allow me to summarize what I learned about the faith from the Fathers: the work of Christ is the starting point for the entire Christian faith. It stands at the center of the Christian view of reality. Both the past and the future are understood through it. Both sin and redemption are interpreted by it.

The victory of Christ over evil is the place where the Christian tradition begins its understanding of the world. That tradition starts with Christ, with the historical event of his death and resurrection. Then, through Christ, it interprets all other aspects of the Christian faith. I believe this over-arching, all-encompassing hope has the power to renew the church. I have seen how this truth brings new life to the experience of worship, spirituality, and to the church's mission to the world.

3
CHRIST AND THE TAPESTRY OF FAITH

The *Christus Victor* theme of the work of Christ was central to the Christian vision of reality in the early church. It did not stand alone. Rather, it was connected to all other aspects of the Christian faith as the central thread to the entire tapestry.

Let me go back to my illustration of the sand castle. I want to indicate what I will develop in the rest of this book in showing how the work of Christ relates to rebuilding God's creation.

In Section Two I will discuss the relationship between Christ and the church. I used to view the church as a collection of individuals who believe in Jesus. I now see how the church fits into the whole story of the universe. I see the church in the context of the story of creation, fall, incarnation, death, resurrection, ascension, and consummation of the age. I now see the church as the *life of that story* in the world. The church is the new creation, made up of the people who constitute the beginning again of the created order.

The church is the new society, the people of the future living in the present, the people of the *Christus Victor,* the people who are defined by the living, dying, rising, and coming again of Christ. All Christian truth that flows from Christ converges in the church. Worship, Scripture, theology, spirituality, education, evangelism, social action, and authority—all belong to the church, and all are defined by the work of Christ. Thus, the church is the community in which the vision of a renewed world is anticipated and experienced.

In Section Three I will discuss the relationship between Christ and worship. For me, worship never really fell together until I first grasped the meaning of Christ's victory over sin and death in its more total aspect. I now see worship as the church's celebration of *Christus Victor*. Worship proclaims and acts out the victory of Christ over evil. In its daily prayer, weekly service, and yearly cycle of sacred time, the church tells and dramatically re-enacts the living, dying, rising, and coming again of Jesus. In both the preached Word and the celebrated Table the underlying reality is the salvation of the entire universe in Christ's action on behalf of the world. Worship renewal, then, is not a matter of gimmicks, but the recovery of the Christian vision of reality, which is being celebrated.

In Section Four I will discuss the relationship between Christ and spirituality. I've always struggled with the meaning of spirituality. I now believe that true spirituality draws its life from the power of *Christus Victor*. This kind of spirituality negates self for the purpose of embracing communion in Christ; it affirms that the world is redeemed through the life of servanthood.

In this way spirituality is a participation in Christ's victory over sin that results in a commitment to witness against the powers of evil. The church, worship, and Scripture are the foci of spirituality while evangelism, teaching, and social action are spirituality's fruits. Therefore, the hope of the spiritual life is the restoration of all things through Christ.

In Section Five I will discuss the relationship between Christ and the mission of the church. In traditional Christian thought the mission of the church is threefold: evangelism, education, and social action. I now see that even each of these aspects of mission is rooted in Christ's victory over sin and death.

Evangelism defies the claim of Satan, confounds the

power of evil, and brings new creation into the life of an individual. It is an evangelism into the ongoing life of Christ in the church, its ministries, and mission.

Education forms the convert by the Christian vision of reality. This formation takes place in the context of community through the celebration of worship and the guidance of the Scriptures, and it results in participation in the mission of the church to the world.

Social action, rooted in *Christus Victor,* applies the victory of Christ over the powers of evil to nature, to society, and to society's institutions. Social action is the work of the church, prompted by the hope of a restored world.

In Section Six I will discuss the relationship between Christ and authority. I will argue that the final authority over all things is Jesus Christ; he gained his authority by virtue of his victory over the powers of evil.

So what is the role of the Bible? you may ask. The Bible is *the authoritative source for the interpretation of Christ.* The Bible is the servant of Christ, for it witnesses to the work of Christ and invites us to interpret our lives and the life of the world by that work.

What about the creeds and theology? How authoritative are they? I will argue that the creed is a witness to the redemptive story that sweeps from creation to consummation. The center of that story is Christ, and the true function of theology is to witness to Christ and to bring us to worship God.

Conclusion

In the Introduction to this section, I described how, as a child, I always looked for the central piece of the puzzle (the same principle also applies to the central thread of a tapestry). *There is also a centerpiece in the Christian faith. And that center, that focal point around which everything else is gathered, is the work of Christ.*

In this Section I have shared with you how the Fathers took me back to the biblical idea that the victory of Christ over evil results in the *recapitulation*. His victory over evil is the key not only to the early Christian tradition but to the renewal of our personal faith, and to the renewal of the life of the church. I want to show how every aspect of the Christian life relates to Christ's victory over the power of evil and to the ultimate renewal of all things.

The early church saw how faith centers in Christ. For them faith did not begin with the church, with worship, with Scripture, with theology, with spirituality, with education, with evangelism or social action. All these aspects of Christianity, important as they were, were servants of this central theme of the Scriptures: *Christ became one of us in order to destroy the power of evil and restore us and the world to its original condition.*

I am firmly convinced that our whole life can be changed when we rediscover this radical vision of the work of Christ. A fuller view of Christ's work will form our vision of life and our acting out of that vision in the here and now. I believe the rediscovery of this vision is transforming the renewing congregations of our time. In this emerging church, whether Catholic, mainline Protestant, evangelical, or charismatic, the centrality of Christ's victory over the power of evil is the dynamic that breathes new life into the church.

Now let's assume for a moment that we rediscover the centrality of the work of Christ. What can we expect to happen in our own lives and in the life of the church? I believe the church will become characterized by a stronger sense of community—the people of God's victory over evil. This sense will result in a feeling of belongingness to the church universal as well as a sense of commitment to the local church. Worship will break through the barriers of passivity as we truly learn how to celebrate Christ's victory; spirituality will be set free from legalism and will lead us into new ways to meditate on the mystery of God acting in Christ, thus helping us to learn how to act in his name; evangelism will become more centered around the local church through lifestyle and worship; education will emphasize formation and not mere information; and I believe our social action will be defined in relation to the powers and the recapitulation of all things at the end of history.

The Fathers of the church took me back to Christ and his work as the center of my faith. And what I'm discovering is that there is a worldwide communion of people who are also in the process of rediscovering a compelling vision of life that bears striking similarity to what the Fathers of the church have taught. The knowledge of Christ as victor over sin and death leads to a personal and communal vision of the recapitulation of all things. Thus, this book calls for the continued recovery of this dynamic vision and describes what it looks like where it is taking place.

If you have not experienced this renewed vision of faith, I invite you to be open to its power to lift your Christian experience into new realms of joy. If you have experienced it, but don't understand it, I urge you to let the Fathers lead you into a deeper comprehension of it. If you sense you are on a spiritual journey, but don't see which path to take, I encourage you to take the path cut by the Fathers. For that path will lead you back to Christ, back to the basics, back to the power and the imagination that gave vitality to an earlier generation of Christians.

He who hath not the church for
his mother hath not God for
his father.

CYPRIAN, A.D. 250

SECTION II

The Tradition about the Church

The Tradition about the Church

Recently, I had the opportunity to speak in a church located in rural Michigan. I knew nothing about the church, except that it was called Countryside Christian Chapel. I assumed, on the basis of its name, that it was a typical evangelical church. And as always, as I have traveled to where I speak, I wondered what I would encounter.

I'm always a bit apprehensive as a speaking engagement draws near. I find some churches to be very cold, fixed, and rigid in their views and very judgmental of those who disagree with them. This is usually my experience in churches that define themselves over against other churches. Their identity is a negative one. They pride themselves on being the only church in town that has the truth. This negative spirit usually spills over into the personality of the whole church; it is a negative spirit that stifles a spirit of joy. So I always wonder what kind of attitude I'll encounter in the churches and groups where I travel.

I suppose, by all accounts, that Countryside Christian Chapel would have to be called fundamentalist or evangelical. But what I found there was an extended family, a family of people that received me as one of their own and drew me into their fellowship immediately. Countryside is only seven years old and has grown from a nucleus of thirty-five people to more than seven hundred.

I asked someone, "Why has this church grown so much in such a short period of time? How do you account for this phenomenon?" "Well," the person said, "I think it's all very simple. We all love each other so much that we simply talk about how wonderful it is to be a part of this extended family." This person didn't have to explain further because I felt it. In the short time I was there I felt so revitalized in my own faith I wanted to stay.

What I experienced there is typical of what I have experienced in various renewing churches. This church was characterized by a fresh experience of the work of Christ making all things new. Many of the people there were new converts. And many others had come from churches that were lifeless or characterized by a stifling spirit. So they were bubbling over with joy to be a part of this church.

What I sensed at Countryside Christian Chapel was a people experiencing a vital connection to the victory of Christ over evil. For them Christ's victory was particularly experienced in the power to break down the walls of individualism. These people were participating in the life of Christ by *being* the family of God in a local community. In more theological terms, you could describe this community as *the people of the victory of Christ*. They were, in a very real way, the new creation, the recapitulation coming into being, experiencing an extension of the victory of Christ over evil in a local body of believers. This is the same kind of experience that the Fathers of the church described.

Before the Fathers led me into this biblical understanding of the church, I don't think I really understood what it meant to be a member of the church, what it meant to participate in the life of the church. Even during my seminary education, I never felt we really addressed the question: What does it mean to be a member of the church? Later, when I turned to the early Christian tradition and began, for the first time, to understand what it meant to be a member of the body of Christ, it was like removing a set of scales that had covered my eyes.

I learned from the early Fathers that the church is intrinsically connected with Christ and his victory over the power of evil. *The church is therefore to be regarded as a kind of continuation of the presence of Jesus in the world.* Jesus is not only seated at the right hand of the Father but is visibly and tangibly present in and to the world through the church.

Most of the people in renewing churches like Countryside Christian Chapel probably couldn't articulate the theological description I have made. However, what I find in renewing churches is this: When I describe the church in these terms—terms which are drawn from the early church tradition—they immediately respond favorably *because they have experienced what I am describing.*

Specifically, it seems to me that the early church Fathers connected the work of Christ with the church through two broad themes: a sense that the church is supernatural and the conviction that there is only one church. I want to develop these two themes and show how they express Christ's presence in the world through the church. Through the images and marks of the church I will explain how the recovery of the supernatural character and the oneness of the church are shaping the renewing church today.

4
IMAGES OF THE CHURCH

The early Christians did not think that Christ had defeated the powers of evil in his living, dying, and rising again without leaving a means by which this redeeming action would continue in the world. For them the continued presence of Christ was found in the church. The church was the sign of *Christus Victor,* the community of people where the victory of Christ over evil becomes present in and to the world.

I find this supernatural idea of the church can be found in the major biblical images of the church. We now turn to these images to get a better sense of what it means to say that the church makes present Christ's victory over sin.

THE PEOPLE OF GOD

The most basic definition of the *ecclesia* in the New Testament is found in our first image of the church, "all the saints in Christ Jesus" (Phil. 1:1). These people are the people *of God;* God gives birth to them. He creates, calls, sustains, and saves them. The origin of the church lies then in the work of redemption through Jesus Christ. Thus, the church is not only the extension of the work of Christ, but also the means through which Christ's work continues in the world.

Like Israel, which was created out of the Exodus event, the church is called forth out of the event of Christ's victory over sin. Therefore, the church throughout the New Testament is designated by words that compare it with God's people in the Old Testament. The church is "a chosen race," "a holy nation," "the true circumcision," "Abraham's sons," "heirs of David's throne," "a remnant," "the elect." Even the life of the church is often compared with the life of Israel. Christians are making their "exodus" to the "promised land." They are "aliens" in a strange land, and Christ is the "bread" from heaven.

The church, like Israel, is also viewed in terms of the future. The idea of the church as traveling to a destination is common in the Bible (See Heb. 12:1; Phil. 3:14; 1 Tim. 6:12): The church is a pilgrim people that has not yet entered into Sabbath rest (Hebrews); an exiled people (Peter); a people who are at enmity with the world (James); a people who wrestle with diabolic powers (Eph. 6); and a bride (Rev. 19:8). The future toward which the church travels is the new heavens and the new earth. These metaphors point to a supernatural understanding of the church, an understanding that renewing churches are experiencing today.

Now we may ask: What does a recovery of a supernatural view of the church mean for the renewing church?

First, I think the renewing church is rediscovering the sense in which the church is the context where salvation takes place. The Holy Spirit makes the benefit of Christ's work available through the church. The experience of the renewing churches today in which the healing presence of Christ *in the church* is being rediscovered flies in the face of any attempt to say "Christ is in, but the church is out."

In the renewing churches like Countryside Christian Chapel, people flock to the church, not because it is a social club or because they want to play religious games; they go because God touches them and brings healing into their lives there. In the church, through its worship, its teaching, and its fellowship, peoples' physical, social and spiritual needs are met because Christ is present in a healing way. Let me give you an example.

A number of years ago when I was more rigid about who should or should not be in the church, an incident occurred that convicted me of my misunderstanding of the church. The incident occurred in a Saturday evening Eucharistic service in an Episcopal church. A man who was obviously drunk was in attendance and, as a matter of fact, received the Eucharist. I went to the rector and in an accusing tone said, "Did you notice that Dale was obviously drunk?" I think I was really saying, "This person should be kicked out of the church." The rector turned to me and said, "Yes, of course I did, and the church is the best place in the world for a drunken person to be . . . the church is a hospital for sinners, not a social club for the healthy."

Smitten by his answer, I immediately remembered the words of Jesus when he was accused of eating with tax collectors and sinners: "Those who are well have no need of a physician, but those who are sick" (Matt. 9:12). Today, Dale is an active member of that same church. Through the church Christ touched him and brought healing into his life.

What was true for Dale can be true for many other people. The church calls sinners to come in through its doors and meet Jesus Christ in all of his power. Christ, who is victor over all the powers of evil, extends his victory to the needy in the church. The church is his hospital for the sick. I now realize more than ever that it is in the church that the Great Physician touches and heals people from the power of evil.

Second, I sense that the people of the renewing church are characterized by a new love for the church. For some reason my Protestant education left me with the feeling that a love for the church was misguided. I was to love Christ but not the church. Love for the church, I was taught, was a replacement for loving Christ. I now disagree with that.

The early church's understanding that the church is an extension of Christ has given me permission to love the church. There is a relationship between my love for the church and my love for Christ; and I sense that people of the renewing church have also experienced the same freedom to love Christ by loving his church. Consequently, when I lecture on the church I always say to my students, "Don't tell me about your personal relationship to Christ unless you can describe it through your relationship with the church."

THE NEW CREATION

A second image that describes the church is the new creation. Something new has begun in Christ. In Christ the old was done away with and a new age begins. As Paul said in 2 Corinthians 5:17: "Therefore, if anyone is in Christ, he is a new creation; old things have passed away; behold, all things have become new." This new creation is to be taken in both an individual and a corporate sense—a new person, a new community of people.

We can grasp the nature of this new creation best when we recognize that the old creation has been affected by sin. The New Testament teaches that Christ is the victor over sin and death. Paul wrote that God "disarmed principalities and powers, He made a public spectacle of them, triumphing over them" in Christ (Col. 2:15). For this reason, "He has delivered us from the power of darkness and translated us into the kingdom of the Son of His love" (Col. 1:13). The early Christians believed that the church, which is the result of Christ's victory over Satan, is a new creation, a new beginning, a new kingdom, a new society within all the societies of the world.

Although the church, as the new creation, is not to be equated with the kingdom that is still future, the church is, as theologian George Eldon Ladd has stated, a witness to the kingdom, an instrument of the kingdom, and the custodian of the kingdom. In that sense the church is the presence of the future in the midst of the old. Although the old creation is dying and will be destroyed (at the Second Coming), a new creation has been born, and is growing up in the midst of the old right now.

A new thrust was released in the death and resurrection of Christ. That thrust is here, present in this life, but will be fully realized in the new heavens and the new earth; now the church is to be the visible presence of the new creation in the world.

Among renewed congregations like Countryside Chapel the traditional image of the church as the new creation has resulted in a new awareness of *the church as the presence of Jesus in the world*. While it is true that Jesus is seated at the right hand of the Father, it is also true that the resurrected Jesus is present in and to the world through the church. The church is the historical people of his victory. They are the sign of redemption.

I find that the sense of being the presence of Christ has resulted in two strong convictions in renewing churches: the first is a new emphasis on social action; the second is a recovery of corporate spirituality. Both are connected to the work of Christ, to the recapitulation of all things in him.

First, I find that renewing churches are recovering what it means to be a redeeming presence in the world. The Bible speaks of the church as salt and light in the world. The early church Fathers translated these metaphors into another image. They spoke of the church as the soul of the world. "What the soul is in the body, that Christians are in the world," wrote the author of the *Epistle to Diognetus* in the second century.

Today renewing churches, whether Catholic, charismatic, evangelical, or mainline, are rediscovering this truth. The theme that the church is to be salt and light is struck, for example, in the Lausanne Covenant, a statement made by a gathering of leading evangelicals, which declares, "The church is at the very center of God's cosmic purpose and is his appointed means of spreading the gospel. But a church which preaches the cross must itself be marked by the cross."[1] The cross was the instrument of servanthood. Like the cross, churches are rediscovering that they become God's redeeming presence by serving the needs of the needy. A biblical and early church axiom was that the church was always on the side of the poor and the oppressed as opposed to being on the side of the rich and the powerful.

Second, as an outgrowth of an understanding of the church as the new creation, a new sense of spirituality in community has been born. If the church is the presence of Christ in the world, then it is a people who are being spiritually formed by his work. We need the church in our struggle with evil. As I write this, the church and I, in my own spiritual pilgrimage with it, are going through Lent. This is a time when the church calls me to deep personal reflection, on my sins, on my relationships, on my attitudes, and on my actions. But I'm not making this journey alone; the whole church is doing it.

What I have in the church is a support group, a whole cadre of people traveling the Lenten journey. Making this pilgrimage together is more powerful than doing it alone. For the people of God are collectively seeking to identify with Jesus' suffering. I find this kind of collective journey draws me up into itself and makes me accountable to Christ through my accountability to the church.

How this new society takes shape in the world is more clearly defined by the next image, the fellowship in faith.

THE FELLOWSHIP IN FAITH

The third biblical image, the church as a fellowship in faith, emphasizes the fabric of human relationships that characterize the people of God, the new creation—what the Nicene Creed called "the communion of the saints."

The fellowship in faith means the church shares a corporate life. For example, Luke describes the early Christians as being of "one heart and one soul" (Acts 4:32).

They even sold their possessions and lived in common, although as the rebellion of Ananais and Sapphira illustrated, this original common community was difficult to administrate. Living together was no easy thing, and the principles of being the church together had to be learned as each member of the community submitted to the rule of Christ. But faith in the end was to overcome the boundaries that separated people—transcending racial, economic, and sexual differences. "There is neither Jew nor Greek, there is neither slave nor free, there is neither male nor female" (Gal. 3:28). These descriptions leave no doubt that the character of the Christian community is far different from the character of other communities.

The difference in character is rooted in a common slavery to Jesus Christ. The image of a slave, so often overlooked, is an image that Paul often used of himself in relation to other believers, "For we do not preach ourselves, but Christ Jesus the Lord, and ourselves your servants for Jesus' sake" (2 Cor. 4:5). A slavery to God immediately transforms relations on the horizontal level. No longer can one person "lord it over" another. All God's people are equal before him and each other. For this reason the church is called "the house of God" (1 Pet. 4:17). We all serve in his house under his authority. Thus, the church is a fellowship in faith—a corporate existence under God, a mutual slavery to each other.

The traditional image of the church as "the fellowship in faith" results in a renewed appreciation of the church as a *new fabric of human relationships*. The church makes concrete a new set of communal relationships.

We may ask how the concept of the church as a fellowship in faith expresses itself in the renewing church. First, I believe the concept of the church as the *community* of God's people breaks down extreme Christian individualism—that practice of the faith that neglects the experience of the community and overemphasizes the personal dimension of Christianity. The community of his people returns us to the idea that the church is an extended family. This concept of an extended family not only has implications for meeting physical and psychological needs but also for extending that concept to the rediscovery of a corporate worship and spirituality (to be addressed in the next section).

True, the Christian faith is intensely personal. "Christ died for me" is an article of faith. Individualism, however, is something different from a personal relationship with God in Christ. Rather, it is a form of Christianity that fails to understand the integral relationship that exists between the members of Christ's body.

Individualism often exhibits itself in a failure to realize the importance of involvement with other Christians in a local church, in a failure to recognize that being a Christian is not something a person does alone, in an overemphasis on personal experience. It devalues the corporate life of the church. This neglect on the whole body of Christ for what has been called "free-lance" Christianity, is a dangerous rejection of the body in which Christ dwells. To be cut off from the church in this way is to be put outside the means of grace and strength received through the church. Faith becomes weakened and ineffective.

The origin of this kind of individualism lies, to some extent at least, in the failure of a misguided revivalism: a revivalism geared toward the personal experience of the individual with Christ to the neglect of the individual's corporate experience in the body. Because revivalism has crossed denominational boundaries, there is a tendency to tell converts to "attend the church of your choice," often without a sufficient definition and explanation of what it means to be part of that church. Thus, certain kinds of evangelism tend to make the church less important than experience and unwittingly support the "Christ is in" but the "church is out" syndrome.

Christianity is not "my experience with Christ," as important as that may be, rightly understood. Rather, Christianity is the objective event of God incarnate in Jesus Christ who died and was raised again to establish a new humanity, the church. The church as Christ's body makes Christianity real to the individual.

This desire to recapture the corporate life of the people of God in the church lies at the heart of current church renewal, especially among charismatic evangelicals and churches that have taken a more open attitude toward the reality of the Spirit in the life of the church.

The emphasis of each of these communities, and many more like them, is to break through the facade of institutionalized individualism to create dynamic Christian relationships. The presence and power of the Holy Spirit can demonstrate a new fabric of relations more akin to the early experience of the church described in the opening chapters of Acts.

The renewing church does not seem to be focusing on the recovery of the local church alone, however. Granted, the focus of community for each Christian is the local body of believers, but beyond that there is our relationship to the church throughout history, including the departed saints who are now with Christ. In a mystical way we are members of the *whole* church, the living and the dead, who constitute the fellowship in faith. The renewing church seems to be characterized by this larger, more comprehensive sense of the church.

THE BODY

The fourth image of the church is as the body of Christ, bringing the other images together and putting the church into an incarnational focus. The image of the body proclaims that "the people of God, the people who share a common life together in Christ, are a physical body of people who really and truly are the body of Christ." It says that Christ is still present in the world both physically and literally as well as spiritually and mystically—in the church.

In Paul "the body of Christ" is understood as antithetical to the "body of death." This contrast is expressed in Romans 5:12–21, a recapitulation passage. Here, there are two humanities: those who stand in solidarity with Adam and constitute the body of death, and those who stand in solidarity with Christ and constitute the body of life.

Paul's reference to the church as the body of Christ is therefore not a mere metaphor containing social and psychological value, but a statement about the relationship that exists between Christ and his body. It says that Christ is one with the church, that the existence of the church is an essential continuation of the life of Jesus in the world; the church is a divine creation which, in a mystical yet real way, coinheres with the Son who is made present through it.

This incarnational motif, the union of the divine and the human, regulated the early Christian perception of the church. It affirmed the church as the divine and visible body of Christ—in whom Christ is mystically present. Christ is seated at the right hand of the Father and really present in the world through the church.

Thus, the body image of the church is that of a revolutionary society of people. Because the church has been reconciled to God, the people of God stand in a new relationship to each other and to the world. As a new order, a new humanity, the church has always had within it the power to be an explosive force in society and in history. For it is called not to contain its message but to live its message, calling all people into a repentance from the old body, into the new body, the new humanity, the new creation, the new kingdom.

A major problem in the modern church has been its failure to have an incarnational understanding of the church. This failure has caused many to view the church as a social institution, a psychiatrist's couch, an evangelistic tent, or a lecture hall.

The current attempt to bring renewal by putting chairs in a circle, singing with a guitar, meeting in homes, and studying the Bible in small groups, if it is done without the rediscovery of the incarnational nature of the church, may be less the beginning of renewal than it is the last gasp before death. Secularism has caused this *atheological* approach. The world has, in a real sense, gotten into the church.

During the last four centuries the church has been unknowingly shaped by social, political, and philosophical forces: Democracy and capitalism have given rise to the rugged individualism expressed in the fierce concern for independence among many of our autonomous churches; denominationalism has reflected the social divisions of society; the industrial movement has produced wealth and, with it, the church has become a landed institution, a corporation wielding economic power through heavy investments; and enlightenment rationalism has robbed the church of its mystical self-concept, so that it has become regarded as little more than a human organization.

However, the change that views the church as the supernatural extension of the presence of Christ in the world though his body is captured in the following words of pastor Ray Stedman: "The holy mystery of the church . . . is the dwelling place of God. He lives in the people. That is the great calling of the church . . . to make visible the invisible Christ."[2]

In summary, renewed churches are drawing on the traditional images of the church as the people of God, the new creation, the fellowship in faith, the body. These images describe the connection between the victorious Christ over sin and the immediate presence of Christ in the church, that new society which is the sign of redemption in the world. The power of this recovered tradition results in a new commitment to the church as the people of God, a love both for Christ *and* for the church, a recognition that Christ and the church cannot be separated from each other, for they are intrinsically linked one with the other. The emphasis is not so much on the church as an institution or a denomination but the church as the people, that community of people created by God in whom and through whom Christ is present in the world. The body of Christ is found in every country and every denomination throughout the world.

5
MARKS OF THE CHURCH

Another truth being rediscovered among renewing people today is the church's oneness. In the words of the Nicene Creed the Fathers declared: "We believe in one Holy, Catholic and Apostolic Church." This confession is not a belief *about* the church, but a belief *in* the church and in Christ's presence in the world through the church. In this sense, then, faith in the church is not limited to a belief in the "invisible" and "spiritual" church. Rather, it specifically confesses to faith in the visible church—the church in history. And as such, it points to the mystery of Christ's presence in the world through the church. These ideas are all very evident in the four traditional marks of the church: One, Holy, Catholic, and Apostolic. Let me explain these marks and tell you how they are revitalizing the church today.

THE CHURCH IS ONE

The oneness of the church is first expressed in the words of Jesus that "they all may be one . . . that the world may believe that You sent Me" (John 17:21). The early church understood Jesus' statement in terms of a visible unity. For them, any break with the church was taken as a serious breach against Christ's body. For example, in a letter to the Corinthian church on the occasion of a revolt by some of the younger members of the church against the elders, Clement, the Bishop of Rome (A.D. 96), pointed to the seriousness with which he took the unity of the body: "Why do we divide and tear to pieces the members of Christ, and raise up such strife against our own body and have reached such a height of madness as to forget that we are members of one another?"[3]

Likewise, in the *Didache* (c. 100), a prayer over the bread at the Agapē feast points to the esteem in which unity was held: "Even as this broken bread was scattered over the hills and was gathered together and became one, so let thy church be gathered together from the ends of the earth into thy kingdom."[4]

It was this kind of spirit that stood behind the more elaborate portrayal of unity in *On The Unity of the Church*, written by Cyprian, Bishop of Carthage (A.D. 250).

> The church also is one, which is spread abroad far and wide into a multitude by an increase of fruitfulness. As there are many rays of sun, but one light; and many

branches of a tree, but one strength based in its tenacious root; yet the unity is still preserved in the source.[5]

How is the concept of the oneness of the church found in the renewing church today? I believe it is found in the way the renewing church is seeking to recapture the early church's understanding that there is only one church. There seems to be a growing recognition that Christ has only one body.

The new generation acknowledges that the church throughout history has unfolded in many forms, and therefore, no one expression of the church stands alone as the true, visible body of Christ. For this reason the emphasis has shifted from separating this group from that group, to a recognition of the unity of the whole church.

The church is no longer viewed as one denomination or the other, but all denominations and groups have Christ dwelling in them. A true ecumenical spirit characterizes the renewing church.

I still cringe when I think of my own former attitude toward the church. I had a separatist remnant mentality. Essentially, I believed there were only a few Christians in the world—certainly Catholics were not Christians; perhaps a few people in the mainline Protestant churches were, but even this was doubtful. The only Christians from my point of view, were the staunch fundamentalists.

I now recognize that there is only one true church and that God's people are found everywhere within it regardless of the label. I often say I'll put Jerry Falwell on one side of me and the Pope on the other and put my arms around both, affirming that we all belong to the church. I believe the emerging church joyously affirms this oneness.

Recently, I was convicted anew about the experience of belonging to the whole church. I was speaking on evangelism in an Episcopal church and referred to a specific situation in evangelism in a way that was negative. An Episcopal layman in this renewed church came up to me afterward and said, "I liked everything you said except your illustration about such-and-such type of evangelism. You see," he said, "I believe that God works in every one of our churches in different ways. And I don't like any Christian group to be put down." I was properly rebuked. And that night I asked God to forgive me and to work within me a love for his whole church, a love which I tell everyone else they should have.

This conversation reminded me once again that the renewing church envisions a unity that accepts diversity as a historical reality, but seeks for unity in the midst of it. In this sense the Catholic, Orthodox, Protestant, and evangelical churches are seen as various forms of the one true church—all based on apostolic teaching and authority, finding a common ground in the witness of the undivided church. I sense that the people of the renewing church find their unity to be a freeing experience. Because they embrace all churches as part of the whole, the sense of belonging to a worldwide community of God's people becomes real and personal.

THE CHURCH IS HOLY

The holiness of the church is expressed in the admonition of Peter: "Be holy, for I am holy" (1 Pet. 1:16). This statement may be understood as standing for the whole body of Christ, for Peter defined the church as a "chosen generation, a royal priesthood, a holy nation, His own special people" (1 Pet. 2:9). While all Christians agree that the church is holy, not all concur on the specific content and meaning of holiness. The majority of Christians admit that it does not refer to a state of holiness achieved by individual members of the church. Holiness belongs to

Jesus Christ; the church that is baptized into him is holy because of his holiness. Christ through the Holy Spirit summons the church to holiness (Rom. 1:7; 1 Cor. 1:2).

The early church in general agreed with Callistus of Rome that the church is like Noah's ark, containing both the clean and the unclean. Pointing to the parable of the tares, Callistus insisted that the wheat and the chaff grow side by side; thus the church contains both sinners and saints. The early church felt that holiness, as a quality of perfection, belongs to Jesus Christ by virtue of who he is, and to his church by virtue of what he has done for it. Therefore, the holiness of Christ's church is not a realized holiness but an anticipated holiness. The church that is "holy and blameless" without "spot and wrinkle" is the one the Son will present to his father. Thus, the church on earth may be regarded as both holy and unholy.

Because people of the renewing church are committed to the oneness of the church, the notion of a separate church that has achieved its holiness makes no sense to them. The old separatist model of "if you don't agree, start your own denomination" has little appeal. Even though Christ is present in the church through word, sacrament, ministry, gifts, and relationship, the church will remain imperfect until the Second Coming when it is made perfect in Christ.

The concept of the church as holy compels the renewing church to affirm the unity of the church in spite of its present denominational diversity. For this reason, many evangelicals brought up in a separatist tradition now question the separatist stance. Many of them are moving back into mainline Protestant churches. And many others, who remain in separatist denominations, no longer share the separatist attitudes of their founding fathers.

Now how has this idea of the holiness of the church as an eschatological goal affected the renewing churches? I think it has specifically helped many people to be more realistic about the human weaknesses of the church.

As I have mentioned, this is something I have had to deal with in my own spiritual journey. At one time I was convinced that my particular brand of Christianity was the right one and that my church alone was right in all the views it held. Therefore, I was hesitant to associate with other churches—the wrong ones, or at least the ones that I believed had a lot of wrong views. It was a freeing experience for me to discover that the church was not yet holy, that its perfection (both doctrinal and ethical) was essentially an eschatological expectation. Now I could embrace the whole church.

THE CHURCH IS CATHOLIC

The word *catholic* was first used by Ignatius when he wrote, "Wherever Jesus Christ is, there is the catholic church." By this designation he pointed to the fullness of truth: the church that is catholic has all the truth—Jesus Christ.

The early church also used the word *catholic* to mean universal. Saint Cyril of Jerusalem in his *Catechetical Lectures* said the church is called catholic because it

> "extends all over the world from one end of the earth to the other; and because it teaches universally and completely one and all the doctrines which ought to come to men's knowledge, concerning things both visible and invisible, heavenly and earthly."[6]

Today Protestants and Catholics are enjoying a spiritual camaraderie that was nonexistent ten years ago. For many years Catholics were taught that Protestants were not fully Christian. Here at Wheaton College where I teach, as in other evangelical schools and institutions, there are a small but growing number of Catholic students. I have several deeply committed Catholic Christians in my course on Christian thought. One of them, a young man who is the youth director at the local Catholic church in Wheaton, has the following inscription painted on his brief case: God Loves Protestants Too. He always sets it up in class so everyone can see it. And, of course, the point is well taken in good spirit. We recognize that we belong to each other because there is only one church that results from Christ's victory over the power of evil.

Bela Vassady, a modern Protestant, in an attempt to come to grips with the full meaning of the word *catholic*, defined it by such words as "universal," "identical," "orthodox," "continuous," and "wholeness or fullness."[7] The church is universal, he argued, not only in the sense that it is worldwide but also in the sense that it is grounded in the universality of the Atonement. The church is identical in that it always remains true to itself in history; that is to say the church is always to remain orthodox. To identify with catholicity, then, is to believe in the continuity of Christ's work in history and to affirm the whole faith.

In the renewing church the mark of the church as catholic has resulted in a new sense that *the fullness of Christ resides in the church universal* and not in any one particular branch of the church. The church catholic needs every branch of the church to be complete.

This affirmation of the fullness of Christ's body throughout the world provides another reason to reject a sectarian spirit and to affirm a truly ecumenical experience for the church. People of the renewing church feel at home with Catholics, Orthodox, mainline Protestants, and charismatics assembled together. The labels and distinctions no longer mean what they once meant. But this sense of unity is based on solid content—for it is a unity of the church as catholic, grounded in a view of the church as apostolic.

THE CHURCH IS APOSTOLIC

The concept of apostolicity indicates a connection both with the past and on the past. It points to the church built "on the foundation of the apostles and prophets," and in this way affirms a view of continuity from one generation to the next (Eph. 2:20). This concept of continuousness reaches back into the way God made himself known in Israel's history. For a Jew, Israel's past is always present. Abraham, Moses, David, and the prophets, as well as the fortunes and misfortunes of Israel as a people, have always been looked on as a present reality—guiding, informing, and directing Hebrew life. In the same way the apostolic church is guided by the witness and authority of the apostles.

People of the renewing church are attracted to the explanation of apostolicity made by the Roman Catholic theologian Hans Küng. He has argued that "the whole church and every individual member shares in this apostolic succession." The argument is that the "church as a whole is the successor to the apostles." The church is not only an institution but also a community of faithful Christians, all of whom stand in apostolic succession in the broadest sense of the term.

Within this apostolic succession there is a special succession of the apostolic pastoral services. Thus, the church, to be apostolic, ought to have within it all the charismatic gifts that were present in the primitive church, and these gifts should be practiced within the body. There is, however, within the many pastoral functions, a specific succession of particular functions through the laying on of hands: the charismatic offices of *presbyter* (pastor), *episkopos* (bishop), and *diakonos* (deacon). These stood out with increasing prominence in the early church. The church recognized in these offices a special authority to service the whole body.

For renewing churches the concept of apostolicity is a uniting rather than a dividing matter. Apostolicity is not found, it is argued, in a particular denomination, but in the church as a whole. The body of Christ shares in the apostolic faith, which has been handed down in the life of the church through the centuries. Those who receive Christ and the apostolic faith today stand in continuity with the past and in unity with one another, regardless of denominational affiliation.

I sensed a particular application of this view of apostolicity in my own life a number of years ago which caused me to change my view of church history. I had believed that the church became apostate at the close of the first century and hadn't emerged again until the Reformation. I can now jokingly (but seriously) say to my students, "We Protestants act as though Pentecost occurred on October 31, 1517, when Martin Luther tacked his *95 Theses* on the door of the Wittenburg church." People who want to start their study of the church with the sixteenth-century Reformers usually express negative views toward the early church Fathers and wonder why evangelicals like myself have a strong interest in their teachings. The fact is that God's church has existed from *the Pentecost described in Acts*. We belong to the whole church and need, for our own spiritual health, to affirm every part of it.

I suspect the Protestants fear that a respect for the early church Fathers will turn them into Roman Catholics. A distinction needs to be made between catholic and Roman Catholic. The early Fathers are catholic in the sense that they defined the classical Christian tradition for the whole church. This is a tradition, as I have been presenting, common to *every branch of the church*. *Roman* Catholicism, as such, is a tradition that goes beyond the common tradition. I believe in the common tradition and share that tradition with my catholic brothers and sisters. But I do not believe in some of the *added* traditions of the Romanization of the church in the medieval era.

The late medieval church is accused of salvation by works, tradition over Scripture, indulgences, and the like. I do not accept these traditions. Many contemporary Roman Catholics don't accept these traditions either. There are other traditions about the Roman church that contemporary Catholics do accept regarding Mary, the Pope, and prayer to the saints that I don't accept. These traditions account for the diversity of the church.

But the early Fathers bring us back to what is common. They stress the work of Christ, the church as the creation of his work, worship as the celebration of his work, spirituality as the living out of his work, the mission of the church as the spread of his work, the Bible as the authoritative source that delivers his work. I'm convinced we have to get behind our various traditions, not in the sense that we totally "clean house," but in the sense that what we stress is the fundamental teaching of the church in its earliest centuries. Here is where our unity lies, and this is what the renewing church all over the world is experiencing.

To summarize, the words *One, Holy, Catholic,* and *Apostolic* point to the oneness of the church, as a matter of faith. Christians, tradition teaches, do not believe something about the oneness of the church, they believe *in* the oneness of the church. Consequently, the renewing church has gone beyond talk *about* the oneness of the church to *experience* the oneness of the church through a commitment to the people of God in every denomination.

Conclusion

I began this section by telling you about my experience at the Countryside Christian Chapel. There I experienced another emerging church, a church that seems to be a living example of the biblical images—the people of God who constitute the new creation and experience the fellowship in faith. This church, this local expression of the body of Christ, seems to experience what it means to be the One, Holy, Catholic, and Apostolic church. Like other renewing churches it has an inclusive, not an exclusive, spirit; and it is like an extended family, a people who love and nurture each other into a maturing relationship to Christ.

Of course, I do not know everything about this church and the many other renewing churches where I have spoken or visited or the ones I have heard about by word of mouth. But I do know this one thing: the ancient saying of Cyprian, "he who hath not the church for his mother has not God for his Father," is coming alive again in the renewing church. It simply recognizes that the victory of Christ over the powers of evil is *found in the church*, which is the beginning again of the Creation. Here, in the church, we find Christ in the concrete experience of being in relationship with the people of God and through them with the victory of Christ over the power of sin. Because of this experience people are being turned on to the church. This new love for the church is a vital characteristic of the emerging church.

I believe powerful changes are occurring today in the church. Whether we enter renewal churches among Catholic, Orthodox, Protestant, evangelical, or charismatic communities, we find a new love for the whole church.

The Holy Spirit seems to be breaking through the institutionalized church of our day, and renewed congregations are experiencing the power of the church in a new way. For them, the church is the context in which the recapitulation of all things becomes a present experience, much as it was for early Christians. What is important is not a list of intellectual propositions to be believed about the church, but the *experience* of being the people of God. What is central is not the church as a cultural institution, but the church as the people of the new creation. This results in an inclusive ecumenical spirit, and a commitment to the church as a visible body of people rather than to the church as an institution.

What this means for the future of the church is *that the church as the people of God will take precedence over the church as a denominational institution*. We can expect denominational loyalties to decline as loyalty to the whole church as the people of God increases. Already many people in the renewing church have jumped denominational lines several times. A typical renewing church of any denomination is likely to have people within it from a half-dozen or more denominational traditions. What they gather around is their relationship with each other in Christ, frequently looking upon denominational doctrinal specifics as curious features of the past. What unites people in the renewing church is community, Bible study, worship, spirituality, and mission, not the emphasis of a particular doctrine.

In renewing churches the people are characterized by a strong sense of commitment to each other. The church is an extended family characterized by a strong emotional bonding and a sharing of time, talent, and finances. The emphasis is on quality of relationships, social involvement with the community, and growth through multiplication of smaller communities. It is in this way that the Spirit seems to be doing a new work in the church of our time. We are being called by the Spirit to return to the tradition of the church—a tradition that emphasizes the supernatural nature of the church and its oneness.

As this piece of bread was scattered over the hills and then was brought together and made one, so let your church be brought together from the ends of the earth into your Kingdom. For yours is the glory and the power through Jesus Christ forever.

A PRAYER FROM THE *DIDACHE*, A.D. 100

SECTION III

The Tradition about Worship

The Tradition about Worship

Recently, I was invited to give two lectures on worship to the southwest division of the Evangelical Theological Society, an organization that brings evangelical theologians together to discuss the trends of thought in biblical and theological interpretation.

I was particularly pleased to have this opportunity to summarize my understanding of biblical-historical insights on worship to a group of my peers. As I traveled there, I wondered what kind of reception the teachings of the early church on worship would receive from these critical minds. I was more than pleasantly surprised by the strong interest I found and the credence these theologians gave to the thinking of the early church. A number of them indicated that they themselves were rediscovering the Fathers of the church and were keenly interested in how the classical Christian tradition could be applied to the church today.

But there was one notable exception. After my lectures were finished, one man stood up and gave a passionate plea for me to forsake my interest in the early church and return, as he said, "to the truth" regarding worship. His speech, which was more like a short sermon, provided us with the opportunity to get to the basics. What is the real problem that many people are experiencing in Protestant worship? What kind of help can the early church Fathers give us in our quest to become worshiping communities? I'd like to answer both of these questions.

To begin with, what kinds of problems do we face in our Protestant communities of worship? As this question was discussed at the theological society, two striking concerns emerged again and again: Protestant worship is too man-centered, and it lacks content.

First, the man-centered nature of worship is expressed either in an overemphasis on reaching the mind of the worshiper or in an overemphasis on triggering an emotional response in the worshiper.

The overemphasis on the intellectual side of worship is committed when the thrust of worship is educational. Here the sermon is central. Everything else is geared around the sermon in a somewhat preliminary fashion. For example, once when I was acting as an interim pastor, a visiting dignitary asked me to "cut down the preliminaries" because, as he said, "I have a lot to say and need as much time as I can get."

No one wants to deny the importance of preaching, for it is through preaching that God addresses his people. But worship that is oriented almost exclusively around preaching results in a loss of balance between God's addressing his people and his people's addressing him. It turns worship into a one-way communication, which in the end is a denial of true worship.

On the other hand, an overemphasis on the emotional side of worship occurs when the service aims to elicit an emotional response. In this situation the invitation usually is central. The music, the testimonies, and the sermon are all designed to lead to the climax of the service, the invitation. People are asked to respond by accepting Christ, by coming forward for baptism, by accepting a call to Christian service, or by rededicating their lives. Of course no evangelical would want to deny the activity of response as a vital aspect of worship, but when the *entire service* is geared toward the response of the congregation at the invitation, the essence of true worship is missed.

The second problem with Protestant worship is that it lacks content; this problem is closely related to the first problem of man-centeredness. A man-centered approach to worship often occurs as a result of a failure to understand *why* content is necessary in worship, *what* the content should include, and *how* the content should be put together.

To begin with, there are some who fail to recognize why content is necessary. We all agree that worship is not contentless. For that reason those who emphasize worship as a teaching ministry are strongly content-oriented. Sermons often are expositions of biblical texts—in many cases a series of sermons explicating a book of the Bible or a theme within the Bible. But while the concern for content in Bible-oriented churches is certainly commendable, the focus is distorted when the content centers almost exclusively on the sermon, which, no matter how deep, can never present all the content that a full service of worship ought to contain.

Thus, the historic Christian approach to worship that emphasizes the adoration of the Father through the Son has been replaced in some churches by a program with a stage and an audience. And the nature of worship as an offering up of the whole person, the entire community, the body through its head, Jesus Christ, as a ministry of praise to the Father, has been replaced by an emphasis that sees the minister as the agent of God to evangelize the lost and to teach the saints. While evangelism and teaching are integral functions of the church, they should not constitute the sum and substance of worship.

Renewing churches are breaking away from the old patterns of sermon-oriented or evangelistically oriented services to rediscover *that in a full service of worship the entire spectrum of the Christian faith is celebrated. They are discovering that worship is a rehearsal of who God is and what he has done that gives expression to the relationship that exists between God and his people.* This is the kind of worship the early church experienced—a worship which I believe to be thoroughly evangelical.

We turn now to the early church to look at their understanding of worship and to address how the rediscovery of early Christian worship shapes the worship of renewing congregations today.

6
REDISCOVERING THE WORSHIP OF THE EARLY CHURCH

In order to understand early Christian worship I want to present a summary of both the form and meaning of worship. These two concerns go to the heart of what the early church did and give us the direction we need for worship renewal.

REDISCOVERING THE FORM OF EARLY CHRISTIAN WORSHIP

The earliest description of Christian worship is found in Acts 2:42. According to Luke the early Christians continued "steadfastly in the apostle's doctrine and fellowship, in the breaking of bread, and in prayers." Liturgical scholarship recognizes that a twofold form of worship is described in this verse: the gathering around the apostolic teaching and the breaking of bread. In brief, the primitive form of worship centered around Word and Table in the context of prayer and fellowship.

The same pattern of worship is found in the earliest noncanonical description of worship, written by Justin Martyr in A.D. 150:

And on the day called Sunday, all who live in cities or in the country gather together to one place, and the memoirs of the apostles or the writings of the prophets are read, as long as time permits; then, when the reader has ceased, the president verbally instructs, and exhorts to the imitation of these good things. Then we all rise together and pray, and, as we before said, when our prayer is ended, bread and wine and water are brought, and the president in like manner offers prayers and thanksgivings, according to his ability, and the people assent, saying Amen; and there is a distribution to each, and a participation of that over which thanks have been given, and to those who are absent a portion is sent by the deacons.[1]

Like Acts 2:42, Justin's summary of early worship consisted of two parts: the liturgy of the Word and the liturgy of the Eucharist. The arrangement of these two parts of worship were as follows:

I. Liturgy of the Word
   Lessons from the Old and New Testaments
   Sermon
   Prayers
   Psalms (not mentioned in this account)
II. Liturgy of the Eucharist
   Kiss of peace (not mentioned in this account)
   Offering of bread, wine, and water
   Prayers and thanksgiving over the bread and wine
   Remembrance of Christ's death (including the narrative of the institution of the Last Supper, and a command to continue in it)
   Amen (said by all the people)
   Communion (reserved portions taken by the deacons to those absent)

Over the years liturgical scholars have debated the origins of these two aspects of a single worship service in the early church. A brief explanation of these origins will help us to understand how important they are to our worship today and where they came from.

THE ORIGIN OF THE LITURGY OF THE WORD

The bulk of scholarship agrees that the service of the word originated from the influence of the worship center of early Jewish Christians, the synagogue. Liturgical scholars have also shown that the four essential elements of the liturgy of the Word—readings from the Holy Scriptures, sermons, prayers, and the singing of psalms—were all adapted from the Jewish synagogue worship.

References to the reading of Scripture in Christian worship are common in literature of the third century. The reader, as in the synagogue, usually went up to the reading desk *(pulpitum)* and read from the Old Testament, the Gospels, and the Epistles. Likewise the custom of expounding from the Scriptures was derived directly from the synagogue. Even the custom of inviting a visitor or a member of the congregation (as in the case of Jesus at Nazareth) to read and to speak was not uncommon among early Christian congregations.

The earliest recorded Christian prayers are also reminiscent of the synagogue, especially in general content and sometimes in language. Prayers calling on God for help, for healing the sick, for forgiveness, and for peace show similarity in wording. But an even greater parallel is found in the subjects of the prayers. Christians prayed for faith, peace, forbearance, self-control, purity, and temperance. Christians were told by Polycarp (c. A.D. 70–155) to pray for "kings, potentates and princes, and for those that persecute and hate you, and for the enemies of the cross." All these, except for the last, were objects of prayer in the synagogue.[2]

The Jewish liturgical use of psalms was also continued in the church as evidenced by 1 Corinthians 14:26: "When you come together, each one has a hymn" (NIV); "speaking to one another in psalms and hymns and spiritual songs" (Eph. 5:19). Pliny, in his letter to the Emperor Trajan in A.D. 110, makes reference to the antiphonal singing of Christians. And according to Ruth Messenger in her pamphlet "Christian Hymns of the First Three Centuries," psalms "formed the bulk of Christian hymnody" in the early centuries of the church.[3]

We may conclude

> "the earliest Christian communities continued the traditional mode of worship to which they had become accustomed in the synagogue . . . so that when the time came for these communities to construct a liturgy of their own, it would be the most natural thing in the world for them to be influenced by the form and thought of their traditional liturgy with which they were so familiar."[4]

THE ORIGIN OF THE LITURGY OF THE EUCHARIST

The second half of early Christian worship, known as the liturgy of the Eucharist (thanksgiving), was also rooted in Judaism as Frank Gavin demonstrated in his work *The Jewish Antecedents of the Christian Sacraments*. Gavin traced the Jewish origin of the Christian thanksgiving to the "blessing of the table," the Jewish grace at meals that included the invocation of the divine name, the expression of thanks, and the act of blessing God for the food. These elements of thanksgiving were part of the Last Supper, which Jesus celebrated with his disciples on the eve of his death. He broke the bread and presumably spoke over it the typical prayer of blessing ("Praised be Yahweh, our God, the King of the world, who brings the bread forth from the earth"), then distributed it saying, "Take, eat; this is My body" (Matt. 26:26).

During the same ritual, the cups were filled four times and drunk. The third cup, the "cup of blessing," held particular significance for the Jews, for the prayer said in connection with it not only thanked God for meat and for drink but also thanked God for his benefits, particularly redemption from Egypt. The prayer also thanked him for the land, for the covenants, and for the law. It was probably after this cup that Jesus said, "Drink from it, all of you. For this is My blood of the new covenant, which is shed for many for the remission of sins" (Matt. 26:27–28). In this act Jesus had taken a Jewish custom filled with religious significance and had given it new meaning in relationship to himself, his death, and the new covenant.

We know from Acts 2:46 that the earliest context of Christian worship was a meal—"[breaking] bread in their *homes*" (NIV, italics mine). This Christian meal is linked to the Last Supper through the post-resurrection appearances of Jesus where, in what may be interpreted as a remembrance of the Last Supper and an anticipation of the coming kingdom and the messianic banquet, Jesus ate with his disciples (Luke 24:30–31, 41–43; John 21:9–12). Equally significant, Jesus was known to them in the breaking of the bread: "They told about the things that had happened on the road, and *how He was known to them in the breaking of bread*" (Luke 24:35, italics mine).

Scholars generally agree that the earliest form of the liturgy of the Eucharist was patterned after the Jewish meal prayers: the breaking of the bread at the beginning of the meal followed by the thanksgiving prayer over the cup of wine mixed with water at the end.

The picture that has emerged through liturgical studies is that the early Christian meal was gradually replaced by a ritual symbolizing the meal. The continual growth of the church into large communities made it increasingly difficult to share an entire meal. Consequently, tables were replaced by a single table, the table of the Lord; and the complete meal gave way to the symbols used by our Lord at the Last Supper—bread and wine. The emphasis on the Lord's Supper as fellowship with him and one another, the presence of Christ, the remembrance of Christ's death, and the anticipation of his return were all part of the church's thanksgiving.

This brief examination of the two parts of Christian worship suggests that the origins of Christian worship lie in Hebrew forms. As Alexander Schmemann observed in *Introduction to Liturgical Theology:* "We have here a dependency of order, not simply a similarity of separate elements, but an identity of sequence and of the relative subordination of one part to another, which defines form within the liturgical significance of each part."[5]

REDISCOVERING THE MEANING OF EARLY CHRISTIAN WORSHIP

The meaning of Christian worship bears certain similarities to the meaning of Jewish worship. Jewish worship reenacted the great deeds of God through recitation and dramatization. The synagogue with its emphasis on the Word brought the Jewish worshiper into an encounter with God through the recitation of the Word—reading and preaching. But Jewish family worship—both weekly worship and the yearly re-enactment of the Exodus in the Passover—also brought about encounter with the God who brought them up out of Egypt. Jewish worship is primarily the celebration of the Exodus experience—that event in which God acted decisively to redeem Israel and to enter into relationship with them as his people.

The celebration of the Exodus experience through recitation (synagogue) and dramatization (Passover) is the key to understanding the meaning of Christian worship. The early Christians, in keeping with their Jewish past, celebrated the new event of redemption in similar fashion to the way they celebrated the Exodus. This strongly suggests, as a number of liturgical scholars agree, that *early Christian worship can be understood as the celebration of the living, dying, and rising again of Jesus Christ for the redemption of the world*.

Allow me to take you a little further into the meaning of worship as the celebration of the work of Christ.

CELEBRATING THE WORK OF CHRIST

We must remember that the early Christians came into worship from a different perspective from modern Christians, having been introduced to the Old Testament before the New was formed. We accept the Old because we have been informed by the New, but they accepted the New because they had been informed by the Old. As Alexander Schmemann remarked, "They believed in the New because they had seen, experienced and perceived the fulfillment of the Old. Jesus was the Christ; the Messiah; the One in whom all the promises and prophecies of the Old Testament were fulfilled."[6]

The earliest Christians, then, saw the coming of Jesus as the fulfillment of their worship. Their theology of creation, sin, the redemption of Israel out of Egypt, and the covenantal relationship they had with God found new meaning in Jesus Christ. Christ did not abolish the Old, but fulfilled it by actualizing it in himself. Salvation was an accomplished fact. History had come to its unique turning point. Therefore, the worship of the church became the fundamental expression of the content of both the old and the new covenants.

The Old, which anticipates the New, was preserved in the liturgy of the Word, and the New, which fulfills the Old, was expressed in the liturgy of the Eucharist, the remembrance of Christ's death and resurrection that inaugurated the New: both Word and sacrament celebrated Jesus Christ and his work of redemption.

Now I want to comment on how the work of redemption, which worship celebrates, extends back to creation, reaches forward to the anticipation of the new heavens and the new earth, rehearses the covenant, and brings glory to the Father. Let me briefly explain the intricacies of this part of the early Christian tapestry that relate worship to the whole Christian vision of reality.

First, celebrating the work of Christ in worship extends back to creation. In Revelation 4:11 the elders worship God because all things exist and were created by his will. The fourth commandment, which instructs Israel to set aside one day of worship to remember God's act of creation, implies that all of life is sacred, that Israel is to live worshipfully toward God in every aspect of life. The whole of life—eating, drinking, sleeping, working, studying, loving, and playing—relates to God.

Creation affirms that life is more than what we see, feel, touch, taste, and smell. There is an interiority to the universe that provokes a worshipful position toward the Creator. For this reason, God set aside one day to be a sign of his lordship over all our time and our activity. Through it we recognize God's rightful claim to every moment of our lives.

Furthermore, in worship the creation itself is set free to worship. First, the work of Jesus Christ is a victory over the powers of evil that rage in the creation and a promise that creation will be delivered from its "bondage to decay." Worship, which is a glimpse of that ultimate *Shalom* (peace), is therefore the context in which the creation itself worships. In worship tangible signs and symbols, chiefly the bread and the wine, are the material signs of creation through which the meaning of Christ's work in the re-creation of the whole universe testifies. Second, worship also reaches forward to the new heaven and the new earth, which are the result of Christ's victory over sin.

Worship proclaims the promise of the total recapitulation of all things, not only in the Word but also at the Table. The bread and wine are special symbols of the messianic banquet.

In a sense the drama of our earthly worship already participates in the promise of the gospel, for the church is called to live out the vision of a redeemed world foreshadowed in our worship. In worship we partially experience the day of his coming through our adoration of the triune God and our experience of the unity of heaven and earth.

Third, the work of Christ celebrated in worship is a rehearsal of the covenantal relationship he has established with us. Revelation 5:10 ascribes worship to the Almighty because he has made his people to be "kings and priests to our God." At Mount Sinai God entered into a covenantal relationship with Israel, sealed with blood. They became "a holy people to the LORD . . . chosen . . . to be a people for Himself" (Deut. 7:6). The Lord became Israel's God, and Israel became God's special people. And in this relationship there emerged tangible signs of that union— the sanctuary, the priesthood, the offerings, and the appointed feasts and seasons.

In the New Testament there is another covenant, sealed with the blood of Christ, through which the church becomes Christ's peculiar possession, "a chosen generation, a royal priesthood, a holy nation, His own special people" (1 Pet. 2:9). This new relationship is the body—the body of Christ, an extension of the Incarnation, the continued presence of Christ on earth, a divine organism inhabited by the presence and power of the Holy Spirit. In the church, his body, there are tangible signs of the presence of Christ—the Word, the sacraments, the priesthood, discipleship, discipline, power, worship, prayer, and love.

Fourth, the celebration of the work of Christ brings glory to the Father. What God has done for us is a revelation of his character. The early church never sought to worship God for his character alone. By celebrating his actions, especially his work of redemption in Jesus Christ, the church glorified the person of the Father. Because of his work for us in Jesus Christ we describe him in the *Gloria in Excelsis* as the only God, the highest, the Lord God, the heavenly King, the almighty God and Father, the Holy One. These ascriptions are central to the vision of worship in Revelation 4 and 5. Here a whole host of creatures, angels, and humans in ever-expanding concentric circles, constantly worship the Lord.

The full impact of Christian content is rehearsed in the Christian community's twofold form of worship—Word and sacrament. Unfortunately, this twofold form became so elaborately developed in the late medieval period in history that the pomp and ceremony of the form crowded out the meaning of it. Nevertheless, the Reformers of the sixteenth century uniformly insisted on maintaining both the Word and the sacrament as necessary parts of a full service of worship.

I believe worship renewal in the church today is recovering both the form and the content of ancient Christian worship—the same form and content the Reformers wanted to preserve.

7
APPLYING THE TRADITION OF WORSHIP

The single most important aspect of worship in the renewing church is the realization that worship celebrates the work of Christ! Let me try to capture the far-reaching implications of this rediscovery by offering several definitions of worship that are behind the changes taking place in worship today. I say *several* definitions because worship is far too expansive to be reduced to a single definition.

First, worship is the telling and acting out of the work of Christ through recitation (Word) and dramatization (Eucharist).

Second, worship rehearses the relationship that exists between God and his people, the church.

Third, worship is a vision of reality, for it expresses the meaning of life and history.

Fourth, worship is expressed not only in our Sunday celebration, but in our daily prayer and the service of our life given to God as an offering of praise.

These are only a few definitions of worship that are taking hold in the renewing churches and giving life not only to Sunday worship but also to God's people in the world. Allow me to show you how these historical understandings of worship relate to the changes taking place in worship among renewing churches.

CHANGES IN THE ORDER OF WORSHIP

I find among renewed congregations, where worship is understood as a telling and acting out of the work of Christ, that there is a *movement away from a lecture-oriented worship toward a more active, action-oriented worship*. In the past, Protestant worship has consisted of a few hymns, a prayer, Scripture readings, and a sermon. The sermon has always been central with everything else regarded as a "preliminary." However, this model of worship is being increasingly questioned.

One of the most immediate consequences of recapturing worship as a telling and acting out of the Christian vision is that a new order of worship emerges. The rule of thumb is that order, rooted in the living, dying, and rising of Christ, which it re-presents, *is the vehicle through which the story of the work of Christ is re-enacted*. The order of worship itself is active, not passive. Order itself tells and acts out the *Christus Victor* and anticipates the recapitulation.

First, a detailed examination of the early Christian services of worship suggests that the order of worship itself proclaimed the work of Christ. Fortunately, for our study, we have manuscripts of actual liturgies from the third and fourth centuries that show us the theological structure of worship. The basic structure of early worship revolved around Word and sacrament and may be diagrammed in summary, as follows:

Here, we have the two means of proclaiming Christ. In Word and sacrament worship celebrates God's plan of redemption. The Word proclaims it and the sacrament re-enacts it; and both Word and sacrament, by the power of the Holy Spirit, bring us the grace of God, the benefits of Christ, when we hear and receive by faith.

Second, the order of worship not only proclaims the work of Christ but renews the covenantal relationship between God and the church. Today the renewing church is rediscovering this kind of worship—a worship that *results in the rehearsal of the Christ event through which one's experience with God is established.*

For example, the preparation for worship rehearses who God is and who we are in relationship to him. Like Isaiah, when he saw "the Lord sitting upon a throne, high and lifted up" and heard the cry, "Holy, holy, holy is the Lord of hosts; / The whole earth is full of His glory!"/ he responded by crying, "Woe is me, for I am undone! / Because I am a man of unclean lips, / And I dwell in the midst of a people of unclean lips; / For my eyes have seen the King, / The LORD of hosts!" (Isa. 6:1–5). To see the Lord in all his glory is to see ourselves as sinful and in need of grace. And that realization is an indispensable aspect of worship.

Next, in the reading and preaching of the Word, God, who spoke, still speaks. The Word tells the story (or a part of the story) that sweeps from creation to consummation. Whether the readings and sermon are drawn from the Pentateuch, the historical books, the wisdom literature, the prophets, the Gospels, the epistles, or the apocalyptic literature, they point to the larger story of which they are a part. The text always serves the larger vision of creation, fall, redemption, and the hope of a new heavens and a new earth. Thus the Word proclaims the vision, applies the vision, and calls people to live their lives in the context of this vision. Through preaching new commitments are made and our relationship with God is deepened.

Likewise the communion table is a celebration of Christ. In the action of "taking," "blessing," "breaking," and "giving" the bread and the wine, Christ creates, redeems, and restores humankind and the world that is the object of Christian rehearsal. This action dramatizes the death and resurrection of Christ for the salvation of the world through sign and symbol and is made real again.

Finally, the dismissal itself is an ordered experience. It sends the believer forth in the name of Christ to live his or her life in the context of the Christian vision. The worshiper is called to "present your bodies a living sacrifice, holy, acceptable to God, which is your reasonable service [worship]" (Rom. 12:1).

Through this order, renewing congregations experience a means of *breaking through the barriers of passive worship.* An order of worship that tells and acts out the work of Christ and rehearses the believers' relationship to God demands response, for it is God's action symbolized in the order. There is a rediscovery of the internal response of faith together with expressions of joy such as the "Amen," the "Thanks be to God," and the "Alleluia."

Other responses are also being recovered such as the restoration of the singing of psalms or other passages of Scripture. Furthermore, the pastoral prayer is being replaced with the peoples' prayer; the kiss of peace is being restored; more responses and music are being incorporated into the communion; and the frequency of communion is also being increased.

A NEW EMPHASIS ON THE EUCHARIST

A Presbyterian minister friend of mine who is a professor at a major evangelical seminary, said to me: "Bob, if we don't restore the Eucharist to its rightful place in our churches, we are going to lose many of our children to the Episcopal church." Many people *are* moving into evangelically alive Episcopal churches, and are doing so, at least in part, because of the weekly celebration of the Eucharist. But the renewing churches of other denominations are also discovering the more frequent use of the Table of the Lord.

The central act of Christian worship in the early church was the breaking of bread. According to Acts 2, the early Christians were "breaking bread daily" in their worship.

The breaking of bread looked back to the post-resurrection appearances of Jesus on the road to Emmaus, back to the upper room, and back to the Sea of Galilee where he ate with them. It also looked forward to his return when they would all eat together in the great messianic banquet. By the daily "breaking of the bread," Christ's followers were celebrating the presence of the risen and soon-coming Lord in their midst, who was made uniquely present in this way.

Later, in Corinth, Paul connected the "breaking of the bread" with the institution of the Lord's Supper at the last Passover. Evidence from the literature of the early church shows that the church always celebrated communion as the focal point of worship.

In the early church the central meaning of the Eucharist was to give thanks (make Eucharist) for the living, dying, and rising again of Jesus, looking forward to the coming again of Christ to establish his kingdom. The motif of celebrating the *Christus Victor* is clearly seen in the earliest known eucharistic prayer of the church, a prayer recorded by Hippolytus, a Bishop at Rome in A.D. 215.

THE ANCIENT EUCHARISTIC PRAYER	COMMENT
We render thanks unto thee, O God, through Thy Beloved Child Jesus Christ, Whom in the last times Thou didst send to us (to be) a Saviour and Redeemer	(The prayer of blessing contained the entire confession of the Christian church. Note that it begins with the essence

and the Messenger of Thy counsel;

Who is Thy Word inseparable (from Thee), through whom Thou was well-pleased;

(Whom) Thou didst send from heaven into (the) Virgin's womb and who conceived within her was made flesh and demonstrated to be Thy Son being born of Holy Spirit and of the Virgin;

Who fulfilling Thy will and preparing for Thee a holy people stretched forth His hands for suffering that he might release from sufferings them who have believed in Thee;

Who when He was betrayed to voluntary suffering that He might abolish death and rend the bonds of the devil and tread down hell and enlighten the righteous and establish the ordinance and demonstrate the resurrection:

Taking bread (and) making eucharist [i.e., giving thanks] to Thee said: Take eat: this is My Body which is broken for you [for the remission of sins]. Likewise also the cup, saying: This is My Blood which is shed for you.

of the Christian message and emphasizes the unity of the Son with the Father, creation, incarnation, obedience, suffering (for the church), victory over evil through the Resurrection, recitation of the institution of the Supper as a remembrance.)

When ye do this [ye] do My "anamnesis."

Doing therefore the "anamnesis" of His death and resurrection we offer to Thee the bread and the cup making eucharist to Thee because Thou hast bidden us [or, found us worthy] to stand before Thee and minister as priest to Thee.

And we pray Thee that [Thou wouldst send Thy Holy Spirit upon the oblation of Thy Holy Church] Thou wouldst grant to all [Thy Saints] who partake to be united [to Thee] that they may be fulfilled with the Holy Spirit for the confirmation of [their] faith in truth,

that [we] may praise and glorify Thee through Thy [Beloved] Child Jesus Christ through whom glory and honour [be] unto Thee and (the) Holy Spirit in Thy holy Church now [and for ever] and world without end. Amen.

"And when he breaks the bread in distributing to each a fragment he shall say:

The Bread of Heaven in Christ Jesus."

"And he who receives shall answer:

Amen."[7]

(The word *anamnesis* means *recall* not mere *memory*, the power of the Holy Spirit to sanctify the elements and the congregation, and finally a recognition that the offering is one of praise to the Father *through* the Son.)

The form and content of communion described by Hippolytus show us how the ultimate focus of worship was on the Cross and the Resurrection; the Eucharist was seen as the climactic point of worship. In the intensity of its focus, Jesus Christ became uniquely present and nourished and strengthened the church which fed on him by faith.

Today in the renewing church the rediscovery of the centrality of the Eucharist is resulting *in a contemporary effort to restore communion to its rightful place*. Protestants, for example, are being drawn back to the emphasis both Luther and Calvin placed on the Lord's Supper. William D. Maxwell in *An Outline of Christian Worship* details how Luther and Calvin insisted on keeping the historic twofold shape of worship. "To imagine," wrote Maxwell, "that Calvin wished to replace sacramental worship by a preaching service is completely to misunderstand his mind and work and to ignore all that he taught and did. His aim was twofold: to restore the Eucharist in its primitive simplicity and true proportions—celebration and communion—as the central weekly service, and, within this service, to give the Holy Scriptures their authoritative place. The Lord's Supper, in all its completeness, was the norm we wished to establish."[8]

Protestant renewing churches are also beginning to *reconsider the memoralist view of the Lord's Supper in favor of a view that emphasizes the active saving and healing presence of Christ at the Table*. The earliest description of Christ's presence at the Table, written by Justin Martyr in A.D. 150 is becoming increasingly acceptable.

> For not as common bread and common drink do we receive these; but in like manner as Jesus Christ our Saviour, having been made flesh by the Word of God, had both flesh and blood for our salvation, so likewise have we been taught that the food which is blessed by the

prayer of His word, and from which our blood and flesh by transformation are nourished, is the flesh and blood of that Jesus who was made flesh.[9]

The emphasis of the early church, as seen in Justin, was not so much that the bread and wine became the real body and blood of Jesus, but that the saving action of God rooted in the Incarnation and the Atonement is made present to the worshiping community through the power of a prayer that sets the bread and wine apart as special agents of divine action. When the elements of bread and wine are taken in faith, the transforming and nourishing power of Christ for the salvation and the healing of the person is made available.

Ralph Martin, professor of New Testament at Fuller Theological Seminary, set forth a description of the action at the Table that sounds remarkably similar to Justin:

> The key term is "remembrance": "this do in remembrance of me." But the church is not engaged in a backward glance and recall as a neutral or detached observer of what happened in the dim past. . . . "Remembering" shares in the dynamic quality of evocation. Past events are regarded as triggering a set of evocative experiences in which those dated events live again; as they are rehearsed they are relived, and relived with all the potency they once had for their original audiences and participants.[10]

Those who have returned to this historical understanding of the climax of Christian worship, where the one who died and rose again is believed to be present and to be received, have discovered the healing power of Christ through the Eucharist. For them, worship has broken through the lifeless nature of what, for some, may be an empty form and has opened them to the joy and accompanying healing that comes from affirming the gracious and active presence of Christ in the sacrament.

Sometimes students or other persons struggling with a painful experience in their lives will come to me for counsel. I always say to them, "Look, I'm not a counselor and I don't have the tools necessary to help you with this problem. But I can suggest one thing—flee to the Eucharist. Get to the Table of the Lord just as fast as you can, because it is there that God can and does touch his people in a healing way."

In all the years that I have been giving this advice, I have yet to have a person come back and tell me it is not true. On the contrary, many have come back to tell me that God through the Eucharist reached into their pain and touched them with his healing presence.

RECOVERING THE CHURCH YEAR AS SPIRITUAL PILGRIMAGE

As worship is being renewed, we are recovering a Christian concept of time, especially as it relates to the reinstating of the church year. The secularization that worship has undergone is perhaps most obvious in the typical Protestant church calendar. Generally, the church year follows the secular year, beginning with New Year's Day and ending with that same year's New Year's Eve. In between, our calendars are full of special events revolving around Mother's Day, Father's Day, Children's Day, Memorial Day, Independence Day, and Labor Day. In some churches special attention is even given to Boy Scout and Girl Scout Day, as well as other national or even local days. This strange mixture of the patriotic, sentimental, and promotional shows how far we are removed from a Christian concept of time.

Some may object to the above analysis, pointing out that most Protestants do have a Christian year because Christmas and Easter are observed. While this is true, the celebration of these events too often lacks meaning because they are frequently entered into with haste, and sometimes even take commercial or promotional shape in the church.

The place from which we stand to develop a Christian view of time is not only Christmas or Easter but also the weekly Eucharist. Here we have, as Gregory Dix observed, "The enactment before God of the historical process of redemption, of the historical events of the crucifixion and resurrection of Jesus by which redemption has been achieved."[11]

From a Christian point of view, the life, death, and resurrection of Jesus Christ are at the center of time, for from Christ we look backward toward creation, the fall, the covenants, and God's working in history to bring redemption. But from the time of the incarnation of Christ we also look forward to the fulfillment of history in his second coming. For this reason time is understood, from the Christian point of view, in and through the redemptive presence of Jesus Christ symbolized in the bread and wine.

Oscar Cullmann has dealt with the biblical concept of time in his well-known book *Christ and Time*. He describes another way of rendering time meaningfully through the Christian concept of eschatology, for the Christian believes that history is moving toward a fulfillment, not an ending. In this sense, the Christian view of time is similar to the Hebraic understanding. The Old Testament looks toward the fulfillment of time in the coming of the Messiah. His coming did not render the events of the Old Testament meaningless, and especially here we may think of the Hebrew sacred year, but by fulfilling them he established their meaning. In the same way the Christian believes that the end of time will fulfill and complete the life, death, and resurrection of Jesus Christ.

For this reason the Christian year is based on the events

in the life of Christ that shape the Christian's understanding of time. By observing the church year, time is aligned with the living, dying, rising, and coming of Christ. The Christian, in his or her view of time, makes a dramatic break with a secular view of time and begins to consciously meditate on the aspect of Christ's life currently being celebrated by the church. Time is actually experienced as *Christus Victor* time, a time that lives in the expectation of the recapitulation. Here is a convenient summary of time rooted in Christ and celebrated by the church as it worships:

Let me explain how time is oriented around the work of Christ and comment on how this view of time is related to the recovery of spirituality.

1. The Cycle of Light

The Cycle of Light that includes Advent, Christmas, and Epiphany celebrates the expectation of Christ, the birth of Christ, and his manifestation to the world. The gospel emphasis is on the light that dispels the darkness of the dominion of evil.

Advent. The word *advent* means *coming.* It not only signals the beginning of the church year (four weeks before Christmas), but points to the three comings of Jesus: his birth, his second coming, his personal coming into our hearts. During this season the church anticipates Christmas in a manner different from the purely secular and materialistic connotations placed on it.

Christmas. Christmas season, which celebrates the Incarnation, consists of Christmas Day and the following two Sundays. The emphasis falls on the birth narratives, the Incarnation, and the adoration of the shepherds.

Epiphany. The word *epiphany* means *manifestation* and points to the manifestation of Christ to the world as the Messiah. It always occurs, after the twelve days of Christmas, on January 6.

2. The Cycle of Life

The Cycle of Life emphasizes the time of Christ's preparation for death, his death, and resurrection, and the coming of the Holy Spirit.

Lent. Lent begins six weeks before resurrection Sunday and signals a time of renewal and preparation for the major events of the Christian understanding of time. This period emphasizes repentance and preparation, including fasting, prayer, and Bible study. It is begun on Ash Wednesday with ashes symbolically placed on the forehead, an Old Testament custom that was a sign of grief and mourning.

Holy Week. Holy Week includes services of worship centering around the triumphant entry on Palm Sunday, the Last Supper, and the agony of Christ on Thursday, his death on Friday, and ends with the Resurrection, which signals the beginning of Easter.

Easter. Easter is a seven-week celebration of the resurrection of Christ that ends with the Ascension and with Pentecost. This is a period of much joy, emphasizing the teachings of Jesus during his post-resurrection appearances.

Pentecost. Pentecost celebrates the coming of the Holy Spirit and the beginning of the church.

3. Ordinary Time

The seasons described above are known as "extraordinary time" because they celebrate the intense periods of Christ's life and work on which the redemption of the world especially depends. "Ordinary time" gains its significance from extraordinary time, but is celebrated with less intensity. The church has time to reflect on the extraordinary events already celebrated and to prepare for their appearance again as the year progresses on its cycle.

Ordinary time after Epiphany. During this time the church celebrates the beginning of Christ's ministry. Especially his baptism, early miracles, and ministry in Judea are the focus of attention.

Ordinary time of Trinity season. Trinity season stretches from pentecost to Advent. It celebrates the growth and ministry of the church.

Among renewing congregations the Christian view of time is being restored because it is being increasingly recognized that the *sacred year is an external guide that organizes the experience of time under the Lordship of Christ.* There is a new awareness among believers that the Lordship of Christ extends beyond a private holiness to include a person's whole existence in the world. For this reason many Christians are adopting a spiritual discipline that organizes time by the church year.

For example, recently I walked by a fellow faculty member's office and noted through the open door that *The Book of Common Prayer* was sitting on his desk. I jokingly said, "Hey, are you turning Episcopal?" "No," my friend answered, "I bought the book for the daily Scripture readings which I read in my quiet time." These Scripture readings are oriented around the church year and bring a person's devotional life up into the life of Christ.

Furthermore, the *celebration of the church year as a spiritual way of journeying through the year is an antidote to secularism.* The materialism and commercialism of Christmas and Easter, the two moments of extraordinary time on the Christian calendar, are significantly counteracted through the adoption of the liturgical church year. Thus, evangelicals increasingly recognize both internal and external advantages to adopting the church year. The constant reminder of time, revolving around the life of Christ and the early church, serves to break down unhealthy distinctions we have made between the secular and the sacred. We must realize that all time belongs to the Lord who has created it, redeemed it, and will consummate it in his coming.

Conclusion

I began this chapter by telling you about my trip to Texas where I lectured on worship to the Evangelical Theological Society. One of the delegates, I stated, objected to the interest in worship renewal that drew from the tradition of the early church.

However, I have attempted to show that the renewing church, which draws on the tradition of the early church, is in the process of forging out a worship that is thoroughly evangelical. What could be more evangelical than the celebration of the gospel? What could bring more glory to the Father than the praise of the work he has accomplished through the Son?

Second, I have attempted to point out that the recovery of worship places a new emphasis on the physical, material, and visual, especially in the recovery of a more frequent use of communion.

Because early Christianity affirmed a holistic concept of reality, it continued to stand in the Hebrew conviction that we can see God through the material world, that material things may be signs and symbols of sacred realities. For the early church the most significant material symbols that communicated eternal realities were the bread and wine of the Eucharist. The incarnational aspect of Christian worship was realized in the Eucharist, the bread and wine being symbols of the death of Christ, by which people are redeemed. The purpose of worship, to praise the Father for redemption through the work of his Son, is proclaimed both by the liturgy of the Word and the liturgy of the Eucharist.

But the climax of worship is the Eucharist, for the symbols of bread and wine are the material objects that are mysteriously connected with the broken body and shed blood of Jesus Christ, through whom we worship the Father. For this reason the early church had a high view of the bread and wine and their place in worship as symbols. This recovery of the visual and the symbolic certainly ties in with the communication revolution that has helped us to recognize nonverbal forms of expression. God has not only spoken but has acted. Therefore worship has to go beyond the verbal to include nonverbal ways of communicating the actions of God.

Third, I have also attempted to show that the recovery of the tradition of worship reshapes our spirituality. We are in the process of rediscovering that observing the church year forms us after the image of Christ.

Now, as a result of rediscovering the early church's approach to worship, what can we expect to see happen in renewing churches? In my opinion we can expect to see four things continue to happen in the renewing church.

First, renewing churches will continue to deepen their understanding that worship celebrates the work of Christ.

Second, there will be an increased effort to bring order and freedom together, ordering worship after the fourfold pattern of preparation, word, sacrament, and dismissal. In this order a considerable amount of flexibility for song, testimony, prayer, and the active work of the Holy Spirit will be maintained.

Third, we can expect to see an increased emphasis on the celebration of communion. Many congregations will work toward the ancient norm of celebrating the Eucharist weekly. In the Eucharistic portion of worship we can anticipate a new and creative use of meditative and celebrative music as well as a more free use of the charismatic gift of healing.

Finally, the increased pressures of secularization, along with the rediscovery of a Christian view of time, will continue to cause many churches to return to the church year as a guide to the development of corporate spirituality through worship.

This rediscovery of worship as the primary celebration of the church, the celebration of the event that redeems the world, is nothing less than the revolutionary recovery of the gospel at work in worship. In the tapestry of faith Christ, who is present in the church, becomes savingly present in worship that celebrates his victory over the powers of evil.

Consequently, people in the renewing church go to worship in the full expectation that God will meet them in a healing and saving way. God's presence in worship turns worship into a live event, a dramatic encounter with Christ, a more fulfilling experience of the Spirit's presence in the life of the church.

Christians belong to another world,
they are the sons of the heavenly Adam,
a new people, children of the heavenly
Spirit, radiant brothers of Christ, like
unto their Father: the spiritual and
radiant Adam.

MACARIUS, A.D. 350

SECTION IV

The Tradition about Spirituality

SECTION IV

The Tradition about Spirituality

*B*ecause of my position as a professor of theology, I frequently have students come by my office to ask me questions. The questions often delve into subjects from career guidance to specific matters of theology and the application of Christian thought to practical living.

After more than two decades in teaching, I think I can say without reservation that the most difficult matter for most people to grasp is spirituality. I can speak for myself and for my students as well as for other people to whom I've spoken. Most Christians deeply desire to achieve an authentic spirituality, yet it seems elusive.

I recall, for example, an incident from my days in seminary. A pastor from the west coast was scheduled to speak in the seminary chapel for a full week on the subject of "reality in the spiritual life." When the topic was first announced, my heart leaped within me as I hoped to get some solid direction. I longed to have a spirituality that was genuine. I no longer remember what he said, but I do know that it did not satisfy my quest.

For most of us who were brought up in the evangelical branch of Christianity, spirituality has been defined almost exclusively in terms of a handy list of dos and don'ts. On the negative side, spirituality means abstinence from worldly habits, such as drinking, smoking, theater attendance, dancing, and card playing; on the positive side, spirituality is defined in terms of church attendance, prayer, regular Bible reading, and witnessing to friends. This formula is usually set forth as a sure way to grow spiritually. But for me it led to a spiritual legalism lacking an authentic life.

When I became a student of church history, I began to look to the struggles of various leaders of the church and to the insights on spirituality from different movements in the church. While spirituality will always remain an open-ended subject for me, I do feel that the early church has provided me with a grasp of what it means to be spiritual.

In brief, spirituality in the early church was rooted in the work of Christ and the vision of reality that results from the promised recapitulation of all things. In fact spirituality is *defined* by the work of Christ (which includes the incarnation, death, resurrection, and coming again). Consequently, in spirituality we seek to be conformed to the image of Christ, and we view life and act within life from the perspective of Christ's victory over evil.

For me, the impact of early church spirituality led me back to Christ. Spirituality begins, I recognized, not so much in what I do, but in what Christ has done. He is the one who brings about the recapitulation. He is the victor over the powers of evil. Therefore, what I want in my life is a reflection of what he has done. There should be evidence of the new creation taking shape in my own person. This dual experience of putting off the old and putting on the new extends to our lives in the church and to our lives in the world. Christ's work in us takes us beyond individualism into a corporate spirituality as well.

The early church knew this as an incarnational spirituality. It is a spirituality that affirms the presence of the divine in the human. Just as God was enfleshed in human form, so a spirituality that is from above, so to speak, is fleshed out below, in a life that is altogether human, a life that is lived out in the world. But it is a life lived out in the world in the context of the ultimate vision of reality—the restoration of all things in the new heavens and the new earth.

8

REDISCOVERING THE SPIRITUALITY OF
THE EARLY CHURCH

Before I comment further on spirituality in the early church, I feel it is necessary to describe some of the problems we experience in our contemporary quest to be spiritual people. A survey of these problems will help to set the stage for our examination of the early church.

PROBLEMS IN CONTEMPORARY SPIRITUALITY

It seems to me that there are two ways in which spiritual failure is evidenced today: first, in what we sometimes *negate* and, second, in what we sometimes *affirm*. The failure in negation occurs when the church, culture, and the mind are rejected; the failure of affirmation occurs when we insist on conformity to subcultural standards, overemphasize familiarity with God, and preach a success-oriented spirituality. These all miss the mark of a spirituality rooted in Christ. True spirituality accepts the fulness of what he has redeemed.

One of our primary failings with regard to spirituality has been that we have often acted as though the church is not the extension of the victory of Christ in the world. We have ignored the resources the Holy Spirit has given us. For fifteen centuries prior to the Reformation a vast reservoir of spirituality had developed within the church. Hours of prayer, exercises of devotion, personal and corporate discipline, communal values and harmony with nature had been introduced, to say nothing of schools of spirituality such as the monastic movements. These movements, which produced leaders like Bernard of Clairvaux (1090–1153) and Francis of Assisi (1182–1226), and the mystical movements, which produced such figures as John Tauler (1300–1361), John of Ruysbroeck (1293–1381), and Thomas á Kempis (1380–1471), were largely lost to the Protestant church. Unfortunately, when the Reformers attempted to rid the church of its bad devotional habits, such as the excessive emphasis on Mary, a preoccupation with the saints, the worship of relics, and devotion to the host, they failed to retain other positive approaches that had characterized the church until then.

A second failing we have had with regard to spirituality has been that we have acted as though Christ did not redeem history. The gradual secularization of culture, along with the retreat of Christianity from culture, has resulted in a spirituality of the closet. God is "up there" and "out there." His relationship to the world is seen almost exclusively in terms of the "spiritual" as over against the "secular." God is to be found in church, in the Bible, in prayer, but not in the field, in the steel mill, in nature, or in history. Consequently, spirituality is gradually reduced to something that runs alongside of life and is no longer the central dynamic force of life itself. For some, the spiritual life has lost its connection to daily activities, to the values by which decisions are made in business and politics, and has become instead the "hour with God," a matter of the closet, shut away from life.

A third failing is that we have acted as though Christ did not save the mind. In the last several hundred years Christianity has gradually retreated from the intellect into the heart. Recently, science and reason, philosophy and psychology, sociology and anthropology, based on a humanistic and not on a theistic worldview, have taken over the minds of even Christians. This has resulted in a cadre of Christians who live "with two caps." The one cap is worn in church or in the doing of "religious" things; the other is worn when thinking or living in the world. Spirituality no longer connected to thinking has become, for some, an indefinable and contentless matter of the heart, an experiential, emotional, and all too often romantic feeling.

FAILURE OF AFFIRMATION

The second set of errors in contemporary spirituality is expressed in what is often unthinkingly affirmed. First, there is the insistence on conformity to subcultural standards. The danger here is that spirituality, instead of being free to affirm what the Bible teaches and what the church has always affirmed, is reduced to legalism. The insistence that spirituality be measured by external standards reduces spirituality to a few easy rules. It's easy not to wear jewelry, to refrain from tobacco and alcohol, and to separate from definable "worldly" practices. And while these rules may produce a well-trained "spiritual army," they often fail to bring a person into a deeper spiritual life.

Equally, a focus on external rules fails to help a person grow into a more holistic relationship with all of life. If anything, legalistic spirituality tends to make a person fearful of people who are not part of the subculture; it produces negative attitudes toward the world, and a lack of personal confidence in what one believes. Spiritual responsibility is reduced to readily defined limits, both in terms of what a person may do, and in terms of with whom a person may associate. But an individualistic, personalistic spirituality cannot come to grips with the expanded spiritual responsibilities of the Christian to culture and to thought.

Second, there is a spirituality that emphasizes an *over-familiarity* with God. The recent emphasis on sensitivity, community, and getting to know one another, which certainly has its good qualities if developed within the limits of reason and common sense, has been carried too far in defining the Christian's relationship to God. Suddenly, God is no longer "the Holy One of Israel"; he's just "of Israel." He is no longer the God of wrath and judgment, but just our buddy, our pal, our friend. When you need "somebody to love you"—he's there. When lonely and down—he's there.

These notions, while they contain some truth, have been so overworked and oversentimentalized in evangelical music, poetry, and publications that they border on blasphemy. When a group of singers can gyrate all over the stage and croon sentimental mush about God the Father, God the Son, and God the Holy Spirit, and the people clap and shout and stomp their feet, then surely our religion has been reduced to the lowest level of commercial entertainment. There is neither majesty nor dignity left in our relationship to God. He is no longer the king before whom we bow, but the teenager we placate with vulgar language and cheap symbols. The end result of this kind of familiarity is not reverence, but a loss of the awe and respect due God.

Finally, a new success-oriented spirituality has recently entered front and center. It is now the age of "God likes to do things big and beautiful." "If you follow God," our religious hucksters tell us, "he'll make you healthy, wealthy, and wise." God is now the great psychiatrist who can cure every ill—the financial wizard who can bring money in for big churches. While God *can* do these things, the overemphasis on this "possibility thinking" may in some ways be a reflection on the "American dream" mentality. The emphasis, both for an individual and for a church, may fall on bigness, beauty, success.

Spirituality then can be measured by beautiful buildings, large crowds, three hundred dollar suits, Cadillacs, and a beautiful home in the suburbs. "God does not want you to be poor or weak or sad; God wants you to be rich, strong, and happy." The danger is that of measuring spirituality in terms of wealth, power, beauty, popularity, and acceptance. When Christianity is made attractive, the result may be an exchange of the true quality of spirituality as a life of humble service that affirms real Christian values for Western values dressed up to look Christian.

In summary, the root of the problem of our confusion over spirituality may be found in the failure to understand the implications the Incarnation has for it. When his humanity is overemphasized, a spirituality that concentrates almost exclusively on the Christian's relationship to the world emerges. When his divinity is overemphasized, a spirituality that concentrates on the other-worldly develops. Surely, the point at which we must begin in restructuring a visible spirituality is with the Incarnation and with the implications that "God made flesh" has on the spiritual life.

In the Christian vision of reality the work of Christ to redeem us and the world is the work of one who is fully divine and human. In him heaven and earth, eternity and time, the spiritual and the material are brought together. Therefore, spirituality, like the Incarnation, does not divorce the Spirit from the physical into a secular and a sacred antithesis, but brings the spiritual and the material together in the church, in worship, and in our mission to the world.

INCARNATIONAL SPIRITUALITY

To begin with incarnational spirituality affirms that Christ is our spirituality. It is his life, death, and resurrection that make us acceptable to God. We cannot love God with our whole heart, soul, and mind, but Christ can and has. We cannot love our neighbor as ourselves, but Christ

111

can and has. It is Christ therefore who presents us to the Father, and it is because of him and through him and in him that we are spiritual.

Athanasius, the great fourth-century theologian, captured the essence of an incarnational spirituality in his famous saying that "God became man in order that man may become God." (By this he did not mean that man could become divine essence; he meant become like God in the moral sense.) In the Incarnation God became his creation in order to restore and renew it. The recapitulation of all things depends upon the Incarnation—the divine one through whom the world was redeemed was clothed in human flesh. Therefore, spirituality itself, which is the attainment of the recapitulation both for people and for the entire creation, is at once divine and human, spiritual and worldly, immaterial and material. Thus, spirituality must address both the spiritual and the human side of life, bringing them together in a creative whole as in the Incarnation.

This balance between the human and the divine is not uniformly found among all the early church Fathers, nor in all the early church movements. Nevertheless, it is the norm. And except for Gnostics, extreme ascetics, and certain tendencies among the followers of Origen, the church sought for an incarnational balance between the divine and the human in its spirituality.

Because spirituality is a spirituality *in Christ*, the tension between what we are and what we are called to become seems apparent. The Christian is a saint because Christ has done everything needed to be done to make the sinner acceptable to God. But the Christian is a sinner because God's work of grace in the sinner is not yet complete. The sinner must struggle with what it means to be in Christ and in the world. Thus, the Christian, even though redeemed, is subject to the limitations of creature-hood.

Our best efforts to discipline ourselves toward response to Christ and maturity in the Spirit are always thwarted and incomplete because we are incapable of Christian maturity in the fullest sense of the word until God's work of redemption has been fulfilled in the second coming of Christ. God is both beyond our grasp so that Paul can speak of "the glass darkly," and yet within our reach so that we can know "the fellowship of his [Christ's] sufferings." For this reason spirituality is something seldom "attained," but that which is always "sought for."

Second, the Incarnation compels us to recognize that spirituality is a response to God in the church.

The church is his body, an essential dimension of his existence, the continuation of the Incarnation, the locale where the "other" is made "near." And here, in the church, are the visible and tangible communicators of his presence. He is present to us in the ministry, in the Scriptures, in prayer, in preaching, in the sacraments, and in Christian living. This means that spirituality may take the specific form of a response to God through his presence in the church. Spirituality may take place through the loving work of service, the devotion of prayer, the attentive hearing and studying of the Word, the reaffirmation of baptismal vows, frequent participation in the communion, confession, unction for the sick, a Christian marriage and home, and virtuous living. Thus, spirituality is not merely the response of the individual but that of the whole church. No one person (other than Christ) can fulfill all that it would take to "love God with your whole heart, soul, and mind, and your neighbors as yourselves." But the whole church, of which we are a part, fulfills this more perfectly than any person, subculture, emphasis, or approach. Instead, the Christian doctrines of creation and incarnation affirm that God is immanent within his world.

Spirituality, however, recognizes that there are two powers at work in the world: the power of Satan and the power of Christ. It recognizes in the words of the Lausanne Covenant "that we are engaged in constant spiritual warfare with the principalities and powers of evil, who are seeking to overthrow the church and frustrate its task."[1]

For this reason spirituality may take shape in the world. It may be expressed by the attempt to establish justice, feed the hungry, clothe the naked, heal the sick. It may concern itself with the disastrous effects of sin in the world, attempt to restore the ecological balance, resist war, fight greed, distribute the wealth, or bring reconciliation between people. In this struggle spirituality recognizes that it is not thereby bringing in the kingdom, but instead is acting out of love and obedience to Jesus Christ, caring for his creation, anticipating the return of Christ when the words of the Lord's prayer "thy kingdom come, thy will be done on *earth* as it is in heaven," will become a reality.

Broadly speaking, spirituality may be defined as a life brought into conformity with Christ. It recognizes that Christ's work makes us a citizen of heaven; that here on earth we journey toward that destination; that our journey occurs in the context of our membership in the body of Christ; that by worship our spirituality is continually formed; and that our mission in the world is to proclaim the Christian vision by our lips and in our deeds.

I believe we have defined spirituality in a way that is consistent with the teachings of the Bible and the faith of the early church. This view sets forth the basis from which a wide variety of approaches to spirituality have developed in the church. It is a perspective that allows us to be inclusive in our attitude toward the many responses God's people have made toward him, and thus to learn and to benefit from the struggle of the entire church to offer not only the "praise of her lips," but also the "praise of her deeds."

SPIRITUALITY IN THE EARLY CHURCH

The most striking feature of New Testament spirituality is its variety. While the response is always to Christ and in Christ, the shape of this response, or the way in which it is expressed, appears to vary from author to author. In general, two strands or broad emphases of spirituality appear to emerge—one stresses detachment from the world, the other stresses involvement in the world. These are not contradictory, however, for no one writer stresses one to the exclusion of the other. Nevertheless, the emphasis as a *distinctive* is clearly there. Two examples will suffice: Paul and Matthew.

First, Paul's central emphasis is around the death and resurrection of Christ. In this event something new happened. And Paul described this in words that convey a contrast between the old and the new using such opposites as: flesh and spirit; law and grace; the present age and the age to come; but above all, the contrast between Adam and Christ. We were "in Adam," and we participated in the old man, in the old humanity, in the old order. But now, because of faith in Christ, we are "in Christ"; we participate in a new humanity, in a new order. This new man has been "clothed with Christ," "walks in the Spirit," has Christ living "in" him, lives in the "body" of Christ, and is "adopted" into the family of God, to use only a few of the famous Pauline metaphors. Consequently, this new person is no longer to be a "slave of sin" but a "slave of righteousness," a person who "puts off the old" and "puts on the new."

These motifs lie at the heart of Pauline spirituality. They indicate the transfer of loyalty from one master to the other—complete and full identity that can be described in terms of death to the one and life to the other: "You died, and your life is hidden with Christ in God. . . . Therefore put to death your members which are on the earth. . . . Put on the new man" (Col. 3:3,5,10).

It is not unfair to Paul to conclude that in his writings there is a strong emphasis on the "other worldly." This is not to say that Paul rejects the body or humanity or creation. It simply recognizes that Paul definitely leans toward spirituality as the denial of self, as a mystical union with Christ, as an ascetic approach to life. Paul's emphasis is on the rejection of the powers of evil that rage in the creation. "We do not wrestle against flesh and blood," he reminds us, but against "principalities, against powers" (Eph. 6:12).

Just as Christ is victor over the powers, so this victory extends to us. Spirituality is an overcoming of the powers of evil and a union with Christ and the heavenly vision of a new creation.

Second, Matthew's spirituality is rooted in the Sermon on the Mount. Here is the "new" law, the one that fulfills and completes the old. It calls, as did the Old Testament law, for poverty of spirit, for mercy, for a desire for justice that *practices* the holiness of God. It is this spirit, this action, this approach to life that will issue forth in the knowledge of God and peace.

The active aspect of spirituality is clearly indicated in the sermon, which takes up the commandments one after the other and stresses the necessity to go beyond a mere external act to the affirmation of a positive love—one that forgives and gives. The three essential practices of Jewish piety—almsgiving, prayer, and fasting—are urged on the believer. They are to be acts that come from the heart, not mere external acts done for show. Next, trust in the providential care of God emphasizes that trust in God, which begins in the inner self, must make itself real in an exterior manner in every aspect of life. Unless it does, it is faith built on sand, not on the rock. Consequently, there are two ways between which we must choose. The one is easy, the other is hard. If we commit ourselves to the ascent, then everything must be left behind.

The unmistakable emphasis of the Sermon on the Mount is an *active* spirituality—a spirituality that reflects the Jewish past, especially the emphasis of the prophets on creative love, justice, and mercy. Matthew's spirituality is one that works in the world, causing the new creation to appear everywhere as a sign of the redemption of all things. The eschatological implications of the work of Christ are applied to the problems of oppression and injustice in society.

Interestingly, in the history of the church the two differing emphases of Paul and Matthew have emerged in the *via negativa* (way of negation) and the *via positiva* (way of affirmation).

The *via negativa* has always affirmed the knowledge of God through some form of direct experience. Historically the way of negation has received more attention than the way of affirmation, partly because it provides a stark contrast to the ordinary way of life, and partly because it uses biblical language, especially that of Paul's, to describe the experience. The way of negation is a way of knowing God that has always been impressed with the transcendence of God, his "otherness," his "hiddenness." For this reason it always emphasizes the need for an experience that is supranatural, an experience that transcends the mundane, the business as usual, the humdrum.

On the other hand, the *via positiva* has always affirmed the knowledge and experience of God through an indirect means. Historically the way of affirmation has been less popular than the way of negation, partly because it demands greater attention to the spiritual significance of the mundane, the earthy, the usual, and partly because it requires action within the structures of life, which, in many cases, is more difficult and more demanding than the more passive approach of negation.

The way of affirmation has always been impressed with the doctrine of creation and subsequent emphasis on the immanence of God in the existing order of creation as well as in the ongoing creative activity of God in history. For this reason it has always emphasized the "form" of things, the "imagery" of God in creation. The way of affirmation is the way of the artist, the poet, the social, moral, and political activist. It affirms humanity, the structures of life, history, and beauty. It calls for an affirmation of God within life and looks for the restoration of all things at the end of history.

However, the church has always recognized the need for both affirmation and negation in the spiritual life of the individual and in the life of the church. In order to understand these two sides of spirituality more fully, we turn to some of the ways in which these approaches appear in the life of the church.

We gain an insight into the negative and the positive approach to spirituality in the early church in respect to preparation for baptism. The person is to fast and "renounce the devil and all his works" before entering into the waters. The way of affirmation is clearly seen in the testing of the new convert by the criterion of good works, "whether they have lived soberly, whether they have honoured the widows, whether they have visited the sick, whether they have been active in well-doing."[2] For the most part the early church maintained a good balance between a passive and an active spirituality.

An example of the spirituality of negation can be drawn from the neo-Platonic emphasis of the Alexandrian monastics, beginning in the third century.

These monastics carried on an important tradition within the religious community that goes back into Judaism. Theirs was a *desert* spirituality. It was a movement into the most desolate and forsaken part of God's creation, where, in solitude, they entered into an intense battle with God's enemy, Satan. It was in the desert that Moses, Jeremiah, John the Baptist, and Jesus wrestled with temptation and were instructed by God. In a sense it is in the desert where one goes, not to flee the world, but to go into its very heart, where, in its center, a victory over evil may be gained.

"The desert is," as John Meyendorff suggested in *St. Gregory Palamas and Orthodox Spirituality,* "the archetypal symbol of the world that is hostile to God, subject to Satan, the dead world to which the Messiah brought new life. And as his first coming was proclaimed by John the Baptist in the desert, so the Christian monks felt that their flight to the desert was an assault on the power of the Evil One, heralding the second coming."[3]

Of course, there were excesses by the desert monks. In spending so much time alone, they failed to participate directly in the "building up of the body of Christ" in the world. They paid little attention to the mission of the church. They were not active in evangelism, teaching, or reshaping the foundations of culture. Instead, they were involved in prayer, continual and fervent prayer on behalf of the church.

An example of the spirituality of affirmation can be seen in the legitimation of the Christian faith by Constantine. Here Christians began to assume a role of public responsibility that they had previously shunned because of the emperor worship it required. Now their attention was drawn toward an effort to master the world, to bring into focus a spirituality that emphasized involvement in the institutions of man. Augustine's *City of God,* which posited two cities, the city of God and the city of man existing side by side, set forth an affirmative spirituality in terms of the Creator who by his providence controls history and moves it toward its end. The struggle between these two cities is interpreted in view of the struggle between good and evil.

Ultimately, the church was to view its task in the world as a call to convert the world, to establish the city of God here on earth. Spirituality, therefore, extended to the activities of the believers in church, society, and culture. Every aspect of life belongs to God the Creator, and is his by right of redemption as well. Therefore, the church is called to redeem the structures of life, to Christianize the social order, to produce a culture that bears the stamp of its creator.

But this approach to spirituality carried dangers. The temptation was to synthesize with culture, to accommodate to worldly materialistic goals, to lose sight of spiritual values, to fail to negate or confront the secularization of the church. As a result the late medieval church became a bureaucracy, burdened with the management of land, susceptible to corruption, hungry for power and wealth. She lost a sense of her spiritual mission and stood in drastic need of reform and renewal.

Protest movements grew up within the church to bear witness against a worldly and secular church. The monastic movements, particularly those inspired by the rule of Benedict, emphasized prayer and work. Here was a synthesis of humanity, discipline, and religion. Here was a movement that was both passive and active. They observed the hours of prayer, contemplation, meditation, and Scripture study, yet they were involved in the fields, in education, in preaching, and in works of charity. In this way monasticism sought for a balance between negation and affirmation and became a key factor not only in the reform of the church but also in the transmitting of education, culture, and works of charity.

Mysticism emerged as another protest movement against a worldly church. It stood in the tradition of negation emphasizing the cultivation of an individual relationship to God. It called for an abandonment of self and a purging of sin and selfishness, as a means to probe through "the Divine Dark" to enter into an ecstatic union with the transcendent deity where a feeling and knowing of God can take place. Mystical experience cannot be confined to the early church or to one or two writers or to a single movement. It spans time and includes Augustine as well as Bernard, Saint Francis, Meister Eckhart, John Tauler, and a number of Protestants since the Reformation.

In brief, a study of early church spirituality seems to suggest that the spiritual norm is the balance between the human and divine, the negative and the affirmative, the mystical and the practical, the monastic and the vocational. However, the attainment of this balance is a struggle. One group stresses the human side of spirituality. Another group stresses the divine side of spirituality. And frequently one group is a corrective for the other, a balance to an extreme.

The early church helps us to *see* the balance, but it also leads us into a recognition that this balance is very difficult to achieve. Perhaps this accounts to some degree for the confusion that still exists regarding spirituality, even in the renewing church.

Let us turn now to look at that struggle and to ask what kind of direction the early church may give us in our desire to have an authentic spirituality, a spirituality that brings together the human and the divine as in the Incarnation, a spirituality that envisions a time when the world will be free from the presence and power of evil.

9
APPLYING THE TRADITION OF SPIRITUALITY

The renewing church today is the heir of the historical struggle to become a spiritual people, a struggle that has been handed down to the Protestant church from the Reformers. For example, a brief survey of spirituality in the sixteenth century shows us that the Protestant reform movements were involved in an attempt to bring a corrective into the spiritual life of the church. The popular piety of the late medieval church had corrupted true spirituality. That popular piety was characterized by the superstitious adoration of the host, the witch hunting of the Inquisition, the superficiality of visions, ignorant beliefs about the Bible, the materialism of relics, the subjectivism of devotion to the Sacred Heart, and moralistic and emotionalistic preaching that produced fear and anxiety.

In this context Luther, Calvin, and the Anabaptists stressed the need for individual faith, for confidence in the Bible, for a direct approach to God through Christ. But even among these leaders, there was a strong difference of opinion on how the spiritual life was actually fleshed out. All three groups affirmed the necessity for personal faith and trust in Christ. Both Luther and Calvin stressed the need for involvement in the world, but the Anabaptists stressed the negation of the world through communal withdrawal, refusal to participate in state functions, pacifism, and rigorous personal moral and spiritual disciplines.

Following the history of Protestantism we discover the same kinds of tensions in the seventeenth century. Many Protestants became too "this worldly," too involved in the affairs of the state, too dependent on mere external forms, on rational and objective religion. In response, Spener and Francke spawned the Pietist movement which stressed the need to have a personal religion of the "heart," a religion of experience combined with good works. Again, in the eighteenth century in England, Wesley began a preaching movement to counteract the deadness of the Anglican church. This movement awakened faith in the hearts of thousands of people, restoring both an inner experience of the reality of God and the outward demonstration of good works in society and culture.

Don Dayton in *Discovering an Evangelical Heritage* has shown us that this evangelical movement produced a balanced spiritual emphasis, providing the world with Christians who brought together biblical negation and affirmation. The evangelicals of the nineteenth century had a strong and lively sense of being "in" Christ coupled with a fervent desire to act in the world as agents of reconciliation in the social order. They seemed to have had a better grip on the relationship between creation and redemption, conversion and action, than popular evangelical Christianity of the twentieth century.

CURRENT STRUGGLES IN SPIRITUALITY

The current renewing church seems to be characterized by the struggle to find a balanced spirituality—one, which like the Incarnation, brings together the human and the divine. I think there is a new sense that the recovery of the human and the divine, the negative and the affirmative, the transcendent and the immanent will come only as we regain a truly incarnational understanding of the faith not only in our perception of the church, its worship, its theology, its mission, but also in our personal and collective spirituality as well.

As we have seen, spirituality begins with Christ. In Christ's death and resurrection, as he was offered up for the life of the world, we find the key to spirituality. *Christus Victor* is the crucial point in history in which all other realities of life find their true meaning. *Christus Victor* serves as the focal point through which a holistic and sacred view of life is recognized.

The Incarnation breaks down those false distinctions between the spiritual and the material, the sacred and the profane, the supernatural and the natural. Jesus Christ is both God *and* man, and when the totality of the church's christological creed is denied, we fall into the error of affirming the divine to the neglect of the human or the human to the neglect of the divine. The consequence is the failure to affirm, in a balanced way, the combination of the human and the divine elements in our own quest to be spiritual people.

I sense that the renewing church is struggling with the relationship between the human and the divine in at least three areas of spirituality that affect both our corporate spirituality and our individual spirituality.

The first area of struggle relates to the tension between institutional Christianity and charismatic Christianity. This problem may be referred to as the Spirit without the offices or the offices without the Spirit. The problem of the Spirit without the offices is similar to the problem encountered by Paul in the Corinthian church. There is an emphasis on spiritual gifts as though they exist apart from the appointed offices of ministry in the body. Such a problem arises out of the strong desire to affirm a mystical experience with Christ through ecstatic spontaneity, raptures, and sometimes abnormal demonstrations. In this sense charismatic Christianity tends to deny the ministry structure of the church as the visible and tangible means through which, in an orderly way, the divine is communicated to man. On the other hand, the opposite extreme occurs when the institutional structures of the church are made ends in themselves, as though there is no need for the power of the Spirit to work through them.

Genuine spirituality in the church develops through the affirmation of *both* spirit and office. In the continual affirmation of the two, God is made real. Even as the Incarnation took place in human form, so the forms of apostles, prophets, teachers, workers of miracles, healers, helpers, administrators, speakers in various tongues (1 Cor. 12:28) are the tangible means through which "all things [are] done for edification" and all things are done "decently and in order" (1 Cor. 14:26,40).

We need both form and freedom—all the forms of the New Testament, and all the freedom of the Spirit that is realized through those forms. In this view the church as an institution and the church as a charismatic experience are brought together. For example, in the worship of the church the victory of Christ is made present. He who conquered the powers of evil in his death and resurrection is now at work in worship, destroying the power of evil in our lives and creating us anew. The charismatic power that is the healing effect of Christ's work is made available to us through the material signs of worship by faith.

The second problem is the tension between mysticism and reason. New Testament spirituality is beyond full comprehension and therefore mystical, but also within the realm of understanding and therefore reasonable. In the history of Christian spiritual experience one or the other of these elements often has been denied. This error may be seen today. The current experience-oriented approach applies a mystical method to the interpreting of Scripture. The "what does it say to you" approach can scarcely be corrected by informed and knowledgeable insights based on the grammatical-historical-theological method of interpretation without running headlong into the accusation of being "unspiritual."

Often the interpretations of well-meant personal insights have to be regarded as sacrosanct simply because "it makes me feel good" or "it gives me a lift." Such a perversion of scriptural interpretation desperately needs the correction of the human insight of reason. God has endowed us with minds and given us the tools of reason. The rejection of the mind, whether it be by the layman in a home study-circle or a preacher in the pulpit, is a blasphemy against creation, a denial of the human in the Incarnation.

But the rejection of the mystical by those who overemphasize reason is equally blasphemous and irreverent. Once Christian truth is grasped, the intellectual apprehension of it becomes personal only as we act on it and live by it. Furthermore, intellectuals need to be characterized by a humility that recognizes that what is known is not *fully* known. Paul knew the limitation of reason, the frailty of the human, and could speak therefore of seeing "through a glass darkly." We hold these truths in earthen vessels, and the failure to remember that is a denial of what it means to be human, to recognize the mysterious nature of even that which is known.

Renewing churches are struggling to find the balance between their poets and their intellects, their other-worldly dreamers and their this-worldly realists. Perhaps it is best to recognize that both are needed, and to allow a loving tension to exist so that a balance between them may be achieved in the larger congregation.

The problem is captured in the attempt to separate the human and divine, the supernatural and the natural. In Christology this took the form of Nestorianism, where the two natures in Christ were so separated that it became necessary to speak almost in terms of the two persons of Jesus Christ. But the Chalcedonian definition insisted on *two* natures, *one* person. In spirituality, dualism emerges in the failure to keep body and soul together in our understanding of persons. Evangelism, as well as the approach taken toward growth in Christ, all too often cultivates the "soul" or the "spiritual" aspect of man. A truly biblical spirituality modeled on the Incarnation treats the whole person and is thus both personal and public.

Spiritual growth is not divorced from ethics. Human values are spiritual values. All growth in love, justice, honesty, morality, wisdom, and knowledge is spiritual growth. Conversely the goals of wealth, power, autonomy, and recognition are the marks of an unspiritual person as much as immorality, impurity, evil desires, greed, anger, wrath, malice, slander, abusive speech, and lying.

True spirituality does not cultivate habits of prayer, Bible reading, and witness, and at the same time disregard time, money, or neighbor. There is only one person—body and soul—and the refusal to regard persons as whole is a failure to recognize the full implication of Jesus Christ as fully God and fully man.

This is particularly seen in the division that still crops up between those who want to stress evangelism and those who desire to emphasize the social dimension of the church's work in the neighborhood and throughout the world. Certainly, all will not agree. Perhaps it is better to have both kinds within some congregations. This could be particularly true when the tension between them, instead of causing division, results in a dual ministry to the unbeliever and to the needy. The only hope for a truly biblical, historic spirituality is that we affirm the whole Christ, the whole Incarnation.

This means that our spirituality is worked out in the church through Word, sacrament, and charisma; that it participates in the other-worldly vision, but not without reason; and that it affirms personal evangelism and spiritual growth, together with a concern for human values and justice in the public area.

NEW DIRECTIONS IN SPIRITUALITY

The underlying assumption regarding spirituality in the renewing church is that, like Incarnation, an authentic spirituality brings together the human and the divine. We can see this blending of the human and the divine in at least five areas of spiritual development taking place in the renewing church.

The Tapestry of Spirituality

First, I sense that the tapestry of spirituality, which recognizes itself as being rooted in Christ, and in the church's worship and mission to the world, is being rediscovered. The renewing church is rediscovering that spirituality cannot be divorced from our life in the body of Christ. Since our life in the body includes being the church—participating in worship, doing God's work, and living in the world—then everything discussed in this book belongs to spirituality.

One can hardly be spiritual if an involvement with the presence of Christ in the world through the church is neglected. We cannot negate the church as though it exists only in the mind of God, and we cannot affirm it as though the sum and substance of it is the local building. Our spirituality must be fleshed out in that constant tension of being the church in mystical union with its head, Jesus Christ, and being the church in the humanity of her offices and in her structure of community. We can no longer say, "I don't need the church."

As I have shown, we must worship to be truly spiritual. Worship is the rehearsal of our relationship to God. It is at that point, through the preaching of the Word and through the administration of the sacrament, that God makes himself uniquely present in the body of Christ. Because worship is not entertainment, there must be a restoration of the incarnational understanding of worship, that is, in worship the divine meets the human. God speaks to us in his Word. He comes to us in the sacrament. We respond in faith and go out to act on it!

In addition, there is a growing awareness that spirituality is related to the mission of the church. All Christians are called to proclaim and to live by the gospel. To proclaim it is to stress the divine side; to live it is to stress the human side. True spirituality seeks to do both; it is not content to serve God only by the lips but also by deeds.

By affirming that our whole life in the world belongs to God in and through the church, worship, theology, and mission is a way of coming to grips with the total claim of Christ over our lives. It is to enter into his kingdom and to live under his reign, awaiting the new heavens and the new earth.

Recovery of Balance

Second, there seems to be a new recognition that our spiritual imbalance in one area necessitates a strong counter emphasis in another area. An examination of the current spiritual movements suggests that imbalance in the past necessitated the emergence of the charismatic movement as well as the emphasis on social involvement. For example, J. Rodman Williams, a well-known charismatic leader, in his work *The Era of the Spirit* has said, "He [God] may have seemed absent, distant, even nonexistent to many of us before, but now his presence is vividly manifest. Suddenly, God is here not in the sense of a vague omnipresence but of a compelling presence."[4] Likewise Jim Wallis in *Agenda for Biblical People,* after describing his conversion experience, adds, "The call to costly discipleship wasn't raised that night, nor would I ever hear it sounded in the churches as I was growing up. . . . The church people didn't care to do anything but justify themselves and the country they loved, the country that seemed uglier and uglier to me."[5]

Both of these writers point to a lack which they and others felt in the spiritual life of the church. Their way of correcting the situation has had the advantage of calling attention to the need for the Spirit and the need for social action. And in doing so, these movements are making an impact on the church, awakening many to spiritual growth through the recovery of the Spirit and the place of social outreach in the church.

In history the church has seldom, if ever, achieved the desired balance. God has, for that reason, raised up such movements as I have mentioned to stress what is lacking in the church. The implication of this, we affirm, is that the whole church belongs to God, not just part of it. The particular emphasis of our own subculture, as well as that of others, is a vital part of the whole. True spirituality is inclusive, not exclusive.

A Treasury of Resources

Third, the renewing church is characterized by a rediscovery of the great treasury of spiritual resources in the history of the church.

The primary source of spiritual reading is the Bible. But we now recognize that in our love of Scripture we dare not avoid the mystics and the activists. Exposure to the great devotional literature of the church is essential. More and more people are turning to the great works of the mystics. Richard Foster has called us to recover Augustine's *Confessions*, Bernard of Clairvaux's *The Steps of Humility*, the anonymous *Theologia Germanica*, and *The Cloud of Unknowing*, as well as *The Imitation of Christ* by Thomas á Kempis, the writings of Meister Eckhart and John Tauler, the works of the Spanish mystics such as Teresa of Avila and John of the Cross, the writings of Protestant mystics like George Fox or William Law, the Russian spiritual literature of Saint Theodosius, Saint Sergious, and *The Way of a Pilgrim*, and the contemporary writings of Thomas Merton and Dag Hammarskjöld. All these writings and more belong to the church. To immerse ourselves in these works is to allow ourselves to be expanded by a great treasury of spirituality.

New attention is also being paid to the less abundant but equally important social writings of the church: Augustine's *City of God*, Thomas Aquinas's writings on church and society contained in his *Summa*, the *Social Gospel* by Rauschenbusch as well as *Moral Man and Immoral Society* by Reinhold Niebuhr, and *Christ and Culture* by his brother, Richard Niebuhr. These works also belong to the church. We may not agree with everything in them, for, like works on theology, they were written for a special time and place. Nevertheless, their value to the ongoing life of the church in the world is indispensable. Those who neglect these works do so to their harm, and those who read them do so for their inspiration and spiritual growth.

Meditation

Fourth, a new interest has emerged in cultivating the art of meditation. Meditation is not a contentless wandering of the mind, but a fixed attention on the object of faith, Jesus Christ. Meditation increases our awareness of him and his work for us. In turn this awareness creates an identification with Christ, a love for him, and a desire to serve him. For example, the early church adopted the practice of Judaism: prayer three times a day at the third, the sixth, and the ninth hours. The prototype was Daniel. Of him we read, "He knelt down on his knees three times that day, and prayed and gave thanks before his God" (Dan. 6:10).

Hippolytus in *The Apostolic Tradition* provides a detailed picture of personal meditative prayer in the early church. It was the custom of Christians throughout the day to meditate on the successive phases of Christ's passion. At the third hour, Christians meditated on the suffering of Christ for "at that hour Christ was nailed to the tree."[6] Hippolytus compared Christ to the shewbread of the old covenant, which was to be offered at the third hour, and to the lamb that was slain. Christ, by contrast, is the living bread, and the good shepherd who gave his life for the sheep. At noonday, or the sixth hour, the Christian is to meditate on the last moments of Christ's life. *The Apostolic Tradition* had this to say:

> At the sixth hour likewise pray also, for, after Christ was nailed to the wood of the cross, the day was divided and there was a great darkness; wherefore let (the faithful) pray at that hour with an effectual prayer, likening themselves to the voice of him who prayed (and) caused all creation to become dark for the unbelieving Jew.[7]

The ninth hour is the moment of Christ's death. At this time the Christian is to make a "great thanksgiving," for our Lord's death marks the beginning of the Resurrection:

> At that hour therefore, Christ poured forth from His pierced side water and blood, and brought the rest of time of that day with light to the evening; so, when He fell asleep, by making the beginning of another day He completed the pattern of His resurrection.[8]

That a mere formal repetition of daily prayer may have little meaning is not disputed. On the other hand, a regular habit of prayer throughout the day (even if circumstances only permit silent prayer) is a means for continual spiritual nourishment. Alexander Schmemann, commenting on the Christian approach to time, which sees every hour of the day in respect to Jesus' death and resurrection, had this to say:

> And thus through that one day all days, all time were transformed into times of *remembrance* and expectation . . . all days, all hours were now referred to this *end* of all "natural" life, to the *beginning* of the new life.[9]

I know of a number of people in the renewing church who are seeking to bring their consciousness of time up into the event of Christ which gives time meaning.

While it may be a minority of people who follow the instructions of Hippolytus for daily prayer, many more now seek to bring their yearly sense of time under the lordship of Christ by adopting a prayer life related to the church year.

For example, the church year organized in the lectionary of daily readings and Sunday texts carries the worshiping community, as well as the individual who practices a daily devotion, through the various stages of the life of Christ and the life of the early church: Advent is a time of anticipation; Christmas rejoices in "God with us"; Epiphany celebrates the manifestation of Christ to the whole world; Lent, a time of repentance and renewal, prepares one to enter spiritually into the death of Christ; Holy Week organizes a spirituality that enters into the last week of Christ's life, taking the devotional life into the tomb; Easter bursts forth with spiritual joy as the resurrection of Christ is an experienced reality; Pentecost renews the power of the Spirit in our lives and ministries; and Trinity season leads us into a deeper understanding of the church and its work in the world.

Spiritual Directors

Finally, there is a rediscovery of the practice of spiritual directors. The office of a spiritual director emerged within monasticism in the early church among the monks who needed the direction of a wise and mature person. The principle was already laid in the personal relationship that existed between Paul and Timothy in New Testament times. Theologically, the idea was grounded in the New Testament notion that the church is the body of Christ, that Christians are "members" of each other. It asserts that no one is a Christian alone. The church is a community of people committed to Christ *and* each other, and in this context growth occurs.

The office of a spiritual director is not an actual church office but a function in the body. A mature Christian assumes responsibility toward one or more other Christians and guides them through regular counsel into a disciplined growth in Christ. The ultimate task of a spiritual director is to help younger Christians find the will of God. In the process, the director may help the person develop disciplined habits of prayer and spiritual reading, may listen to the confession of sins, and may encourage and counsel the growing Christian in many areas of life.

In summary, the renewing church is discovering that spirituality cannot be divorced from the human and the material of this world. Rather, it is rooted in Christ and is fleshed out in the redemption of people, institutions, and history.

Conclusion

In the introduction to this chapter, I indicated that the search for an authentic spirituality is a mark of the renewing church.

In the early church spirituality was understood in terms of the work of Christ. Thus spirituality is not so much "my spirituality" as it is "his spirituality extended to me." And it comes to us through the church, particularly in worship where we celebrate the vision of a restored universe. Spirituality extends to the mission of the church who proclaims this vision and calls people to live in it.

The specific implication of this spirituality is found in its incarnational dimension. As the divine became present through the creation, so the divine and human are now spiritually united. The human is the carrier of the divine and can become an image of redemption as does the bread and wine or a cup of cold water given in his name.

In my opinion the renewing church is returning to an incarnational view of spirituality that recognizes the validity of the divine and the human in the struggle to be spiritual. Through the negative, the renewing church is asserting the need to rise above life, to reach God through self-abandonment and quiet. Through the positive, it is sensing that we meet God in the responsibility of life, in the process of history, in the issues of the day.

Consequently, what we can expect from the renewing church in the future is this: First, there will be a continued rise of interest in meditation, contemplation, and prayer. For resources, the renewing church will be drawing from the tradition of the church, both the Catholic tradition in the West, and the Orthodox tradition in the East. Emphasis will be placed on the writings of the mystical tradition, new books of prayer will emerge, monasteries will experience a new life, and a small but influential Protestant monastic movement may take shape.

Second, the renewing church will become increasingly active in the social issues of our day. An affirmative spirituality will take shape in a continued effort to support the sanctity of life as in antiabortion rallies and peace movements. There will be a growing concern for the poor, for the support of justice and equality in stands taken against apartheid and in stands taken in support of the rights of women.

Perhaps, above all, the church will increasingly learn to live in the vision of Christ who conquered evil and will restore the universe. For our all-time citizenship, our ultimate vision of reality, is rooted in the Second Adam who makes all things new.

*What the soul is in the
body, that Christians are
in the world.*

EPISTLE TO DIOGNETUS, c. A.D. 200

SECTION V

*The Tradition about the Mission
of the Church*

The Tradition about the Mission
of the Church

The first seven years of my life were spent in Africa where my parents were missionaries. I still have vivid memories of our mission station located in a clearing within the thick wilds of the jungle. All around us, as far as the eye could see, were the impenetrable forests of deepest Africa.

While it was the jungle that drew on my imagination as a child, it is the buildings of the clearing that come into view when I think of the church in the world today. My thoughts turn to the church and the barn in that clearing as symbols of the mission of the church.

First, I see the church as a symbol of evangelism. The Africans were able to look at that building and sense that Christ was calling them to enter into the new community of faith. And then during the week, the church doubled as a schoolhouse where the Africans were schooled in the Bible. As I reflect on the double use of the church building, I'm reminded of the union that exists between evangelism and education. For the church into which we have been born is also the nurse that nurtures us into the faith and causes us to grow.

The other building on the compound that exercises my imagination is the barn. To me, the barn stands as the symbol of the social action of the church. Around the barn were the chickens, the goats, the pigs, and beyond that were fields of vegetables and sugar cane. Missionaries even then were concerned not only with the soul, but with the re-creation of the world. The work of teaching the nationals how to cultivate the ground, plant the seed, and care for the tender shoots was a work of putting the creation to redemptive use.

This threefold mission of evangelism, education, and social action is rooted in the victory of Christ over evil, which results in the recapitulation, the ultimate restoration of all things in Christ. Here we see once again the central thread of *Christus Victor*. The victory of Christ over evil is the fundamental source of the church's mission. *When the church evangelizes, educates, and meets solid needs, it continues the work of Christ in the world.*

In the New Testament the mission of the church is summarized by Matthew: "Go therefore and make disciples of all the nations, baptizing them in the name of the Father and of the Son and of the Holy Spirit, teaching them to observe all things that I have commanded you; and lo, I am with you always, even to the close of the age" (28: 19–20). The sequence is make disciples . . . baptize . . . teach.

Not only is the mission of the church to evangelize and to educate but also to serve the world. The God of the Bible is a sending God. He sent the prophets; he sent his Son; he sent the apostles; he sends us. The mission of the church must therefore be understood in an incarnational sense. That is, as he sent his Son, so he sends us. "As the Father has sent Me," Jesus said, "I also send you" (John 20:21). As Jesus was sent to serve, so his church is sent into the world to serve.

10
EVANGELISM IN THE EARLY CHURCH

That evangelism is the hallmark of evangelical Christianity, no one can question. In this century alone evangelicals have circled the globe and penetrated into the obscure parts of the world to present Christ's saving message to millions of people. Recently the Roman Catholic church and the World Council of Churches have recognized the urgency of evangelism and are now giving greater attention to what has always consumed the energies of evangelical Christians.

PROBLEMS IN CONTEMPORARY EVANGELISM

Although it is not popular to critique evangelical efforts at evangelism, constructive self-criticism always has the value of strengthening the church rather than weakening it. In this spirit many evangelical leaders have come to recognize that the major fault of evangelism among evangelicals has been the tendency to oversimplify the Christian message.

The oversimplification of evangelism is rooted in what R. B. Kuiper in *God-centered Evangelism* called man-centered evangelism:

> . . . too often the limelight is turned full upon the evangelist—his personality, his eloquence, his ability as an organizer, the story of his conversion, the hardships which he has endured, the number of his converts, in some instances the miracles of healing allegedly performed by him. At other times attention is focused on those who are being evangelized—their large numbers, their sorry plight as exemplified by poverty, disease and

immorality, their supposed yearning for the gospel of salvation, and, worst of all, the good that is said to dwell in them and to enable men to exercise saving faith of their own free, although unregenerate, volition. And how often the welfare of man, whether temporal or eternal, is made the sole end of evangelism.[1]

Unfortunately, there are at least two ways in which this oversimplification of the gospel may be expressed in evangelism: the first occurs when evangelism is divorced from theology; the second when Christian obedience as the result of faith is neglected.

First, a man-centered evangelism tends to divorce the gospel from the theology of the church. Whatever one thinks of Wesley, Whitefield, Edwards, or Finney, it will have to be admitted that they attempted to evangelize within a framework of theology. John R. Stott, in one of his earliest works, *Fundamentalism and Evangelism,* recognizes the need for an evangelism with content and urged that "we shall be faithful in outlining the implications of the Christian life. We shall urge our hearers to count the cost of Christian discipleship . . . we shall preach the repentance which is a turning from all known sin and a readiness to make restitution where possible. We shall proclaim the lordship of Christ and the necessity of the unconditional surrender of every department of life to Him. We shall plead also for an open and unashamed allegiance to Christ in the fellowship of the church."[2]

Second, evangelism has separated its message from obedience. Jim Wallis argued in *Agenda for Biblical People,* "The great tragedy of modern evangelism is in calling many to belief but few to obedience."[3]

The separation of evangelism from obedience produces the cult of easy and attractive Christianity. All too often the faith is packaged through beautiful people who testify that Christianity has really been good for them: It has given meaning to life, saved a marriage and a home, or made life fun.

Others testify that they are now happy, acceptable, in control of things, popular, and even rich. I do not mean to demean the positive effects of Christianity. Certainly many lives are given meaning and direction. Our major emphasis, however, must not be to make Christianity attractive, as attractive as it is, nor to make it a panacea for all ills, as much as it does give life meaning and purpose. Instead, we must emphasize the cost of discipleship, the absolute claim of God over our entire life, and the necessity of a faith that issues forth in obedience. It is a problem of balance and emphasis. The need is to return to the biblical message and its demands.

One reason modern evangelism may be divorced from obedience is due to the purpose of evangelists. Evangelists seek to elicit a response, to get someone to make a decision, to make a commitment to Christ. For this reason evangelistic services sometimes play on the emotions. The music, the testimonies, the sermon, the invitation are all geared so that the emotional level of the people can be skillfully and psychologically guided toward a decision.

Often such a heavy emphasis is put on the decision that the inquirer leaves with the false impression that the sum and substance of Christianity is in making a decision. The result is an individualization of the Christian message. The need for pre-evangelism, for a return to the unity between *kerygma* (preaching) and *didache* (teaching), for a follow-up program in the local church is being increasingly recognized as a healthy corrective to emotional evangelism.

Another reason for the divorce between evangelism and obedience may be found in "cultural conversions." That is, a person may make a radical break from a former way of living into a particular form of Christianity. For exam-

143

ple, a person may be persuaded to give up bad habits and join a group whose identity is strongly defined by the *absence* of smoking, drinking, dancing, gambling, and the like. The problem is that the new convert may confuse an obedience to the forms of this "new culture" with an obedience to Christ. The person may be told that obedience means giving up bad habits, and taking on new habits such as Bible reading, prayer, witnessing, attendance at church, and tithing.

As good as these new habits are, they do not get at the heart of Christian obedience, and the reduction of the Christian life to these few principles tends to obscure deeper issues as well as to lead the convert who obeys them to substitute a cultural change of habits for a more far-reaching biblical change of lifestyle.

Having summarized these problems, we turn now to look at the pattern of evangelism in the early church.

EVANGELISM IN THE EARLY CHURCH

The Content of Evangelism in the Early Church

When Jesus began to preach, his message was the kingdom of God. Although John the Baptist preceded Jesus and had already preached the coming of the kingdom, Jesus' proclamation was something new. The Baptist was speaking as a prophet of the one who was to come. But Jesus was the event John proclaimed; the kingdom had arrived in him. To understand New Testament evangelism, then, we must understand the meaning of the kingdom.

The basic meaning of the Greek word *basileia* (kingdom) is twofold. First it refers to the *realm* of a king, and second to the *rule* of the king. These two meanings may be applied in three ways, as George Eldon Ladd, in his book *The Gospel of the Kingdom* has shown. Some passages refer to the kingdom as "God's *reign*"; others refer to God's kingdom as the "*realm* into which we may now enter to experience the blessings of his reign"; and still others refer to a "future realm which will come only with the return of our Lord Jesus Christ into which we shall then enter and experience the fulness of His reign."[4] These distinctions force the serious Bible student to examine every reference to the kingdom in its context in order to know which of the aspects of the kingdom is being mentioned.

There are, however, despite different usages of the word *kingdom*, three underlying themes which permeate the *kingdom* uses.

First, the underlying theme is the *rule of God in Christ over all the areas of life*. It is this rule that Jesus proclaimed. In effect he was saying, "The ruler of the universe has come to rule in your life. . . . Turn away from all other demands for ownership of your life. . . . Enter into my reign. Let me rule in the life of the world through my rule in you." Jesus called men away from following their false gods to follow the one true God manifested in himself.

To grasp the meaning of the rule of Christ we must take into account the New Testament contrast between the kingdom of Christ and the kingdom of Satan. We see Christ's kingdom as a "rule" more clearly when we view his kingdom within the context of the antikingdom of Satan. It is of primary importance to recognize that the contrast is between two rules in the world order.

Satan's rule in this world is not some kind of ownership of creation. (This is a Gnostic doctrine which has crept into the thinking of many people, i.e., the world belongs to Satan and therefore it is bad and everything in it is evil.) On the contrary, the ownership of the world belongs to God by virtue of the Creation. It is his world and it is good! However, due to the Fall, a new force or power had been unleashed—namely, the power of the evil one *who rules in the hearts of people and in the life of the world through them.* So the conflict between Jesus and Satan has nothing to do with the physical world. It has to do with persons. By whom will the life of persons be ruled? By the king of evil or by God's king, Christ, who is victor over evil?

The second underlying theme of the kingdom is that *it is a gift.* Jesus pointedly emphasizes that people must be born into the kingdom. The kingdom comes to a person without a person's help or actions (John 3:5-6, 8; Mark 9:1; Luke 17:20-21). Although entrance into the kingdom is viewed as a gift, there are also correlatives that look at entrance into the kingdom from a person's point of view. The way a person is to receive the rule of God is as a child (Mark 10:15). The self-righteous Pharisees and other Jewish leaders won't get into the kingdom because of their refusal to repent (Matt. 21:31-32).

The third underlying motif is that Jesus *himself is the embodiment of the kingdom* (Matt. 19:29; 21:9; Mark 10:29; 11:9-10; Luke 18:29-30). It was the king-god who "became flesh and dwelt among us" (John 1:14). It is this king who was made flesh, who died and was buried, who was raised from the dead, who is present in the church, who is returning for those he rules. He is the one who is announced and is present in the proclamation. To preach Jesus Christ then is to preach the kingdom.

The content of the Good News is the coming of Christ— who is himself the Good News—the embodiment of the kingdom. In Jesus both the publication of the Good News and the actualization of the Good News are brought together. He not only proclaims the Good News but he *is* the Good News and he *does* the Good News. He is the content of his message.

We should note then that it is this theme (Jesus—the kingdom) that the apostles preached. Jesus sent the disciples "to tell everyone about the coming of the Kingdom of

God" (Luke 9:2 LB). The ministry of the apostles began after Pentecost and as a result of the persecution "the believers who had fled Jerusalem went everywhere preaching the Good News about Jesus!" (Acts 8:4 LB).

Aspects of Apostolic Preaching

For this reason, there are three aspects about apostolic preaching and teaching that are important to keep in mind in evangelism. The first is that the apostles were not preaching mere facts, but an interpretation of an event. The message was that Jesus lived, died, and rose again *for their sin!* Salvation is no mere assent to the facts about the king—but the actualization of repentance, faith, and obedience. This is the Good News that saves (1 Cor. 15:2).

The second aspect of apostolic preaching is that Christ is the inaugurator of a new era in the church. The special feature of this new era is that God himself has entered into human history (John 1:14). It is the age in which the king of glory has *appeared* in human flesh and lived out before the eyes of people the rule of the king. Because he is that king, he calls people to follow him, to live under his rule, and establish him as the lord of their lives. The presence of his kingdom is within them (Luke 17:20–21) and some day will extend over the whole world (Rev. 11:15).

The full-blown development of this kingdom concept as it relates both to the presence of the kingdom in the here and now and as it relates to the ultimate fulfillment and establishment of the eternal kingdom means that there can be no area of life that escapes the rule of the king. His rulership extends over all of life. What we do, say, and think must be executed under his rule. Our eating, sleeping, drinking, judging, and loving must all take place under the rule of the king. He is the lord of *life*—all of life. Thus the inauguration of the new age is not some mere intrusion into the secular world, nor a spiritual component that runs alongside of life. Rather, it is the central dynamic to the whole of life and it involves the whole person in all his or her thinking, feeling, and living aspects.

A third aspect of apostolic evangelism in the New Testament is that it always led to baptism and entrance into the church, the realm where Christ rules. Baptism was a physical sign and seal of conversion, of a turning away from a wrong way of life, of a trusting in Jesus.

Baptism was no empty symbol, no mere external act, but an act that was a *necessary* aspect of conversion. The message was repent *and* be baptized. The doctrine of justification and the doctrine of baptism were all of one piece, in a holistic sense. It is no accident, as Michael Green remarked in *Evangelism in the Early Church*, that Romans 6, the great chapter on baptism as an identification with Christ, comes after Romans 5, the great chapter on justification. They belong together and the pattern of the early church was always conversion, then baptism.[5]

A brief consideration of the meaning of baptism in the New Testament period shows us how important baptism was regarded. Baptism implies repentance and renunciation; its form symbolizes the main facts of the gospel; its content signifies an entrance into the new community, and a mark of the reception of the Spirit.

The cumulative evidence of all these notions that are filled with content suggests that conversion and baptism were not mere emotional experiences, but were entered into on the basis of understanding. Evangelism in the New Testament was not based on emotion, but on *content*. It was an appeal made on the basis of the truth of Jesus' victory over evil and what that meant for mankind, history, and the world.

The Method of Evangelism in the Early Church

In the early church, evangelism took place in connection with worship and the rite of baptism.

Liturgical scholars have identified seven steps of evangelism through worship in the early church. These were (1) inquiry; (2) a rite of welcome; (3) a period of instruction; (4) the rite of election; (5) a period of intense preparation for baptism; (6) the rite of baptism; and (7) a period for follow-up and incorporation into the full life of the church. Because these seven stages have been fully developed in my book *Celebrating Our Faith: Evangelism Through Worship*, I will only comment briefly on this method of evangelism.

First of all, this early local church evangelism assumed four things. First, it was based on the *Christus Victor* understanding of the death of Christ. Second, it presupposed that the church plays a mothering role in the process of salvation. Thus, the church was referred to as the "womb" in which the formation of the new convert took place and the "breast" where the new convert was nourished. Third, the rituals of the church pertaining to salvation (passage rites) were treated as external means of organizing an internal experience. And, finally, conversion was understood as being in various stages of development; a person was led through a maturation that led to baptism and entrance into the church as the culminating events of the converting process.

Allow me to describe third-century evangelism a little more fully by asking you to use your imagination. Let's assume for a moment that you are a third-century neighbor to a devout Christian. Through that person's life and witness your desire to become a Christian grows in intensity, and you share this with your neighbor who then evangelizes you third-century style (the roots of which are in the New Testament, but space does not permit that development here). What is the process through which you will be carried?

The answer to this question is fully described by Hippolytus in his work *The Apostolic Tradition*.[6] This work, written around A.D. 200, provides us with a description of the life of the church in the early third century. This is not the only work that describes evangelism through worship, but it is the most complete and succinct.

First you will be taken to an *inquiry* conducted by the pastor or readers of the church in what might be called a pre-evangelism screening. The purpose is to proclaim the gospel clearly and to determine whether your commitment to Christ is real. Second, assuming you have made a firm commitment of faith, you are next brought into the life of the church through the *rite of welcome*. This simple ritual had as its central feature a verbal and symbolic repudiation of the devil and all his works along with words and symbols that indicate you are turning to Christ.

You then enter into a period of instruction known as the *catechumenate* (the word means *instruction*), which may last as long as three years. During this time you are taught the faith and discipled in your Christian living. At the end of this period you pass through the *rites of election*, a ritual service that included writing your name in the book of life. This service symbolizes that God has chosen you and that you in turn choose him.

Next, you enter into a six-week period of intense spiritual preparations for baptism. Known as *purification and enlightenment* and scheduled during Lent, this period is a time of prayer, Scripture, and fasting in preparation for baptism. Then, baptism, known as the *rite of initiation*, is administered on Easter Sunday after an all-night vigil service. At this time you are baptized in water, receive the anointing of oil symbolizing the Holy Spirit, and receive for the first time the bread and wine, the symbol of your salvation. Finally, after Easter in a period known as *mystogogue*, you are fully incorporated into the life of the church. During this follow-up period you are given a deeper appreciation of baptism and the Lord's Supper.

EVANGELISM IN THE RENEWING CHURCH

One of the major characteristics of the renewing church that I have been describing in this book is: *an acknowledgment that we live in a secular world*. This means that both the evangelistic content and the method of the renewing church are increasingly similar to those of the early church, a time when the church was evangelizing in a society that was thoroughly secular. After the conversion of Constantine and the quasi-Christianization of the Roman Empire, the methods of evangelism underwent some significant changes. And now, with the increasing recognition that American society is not really Christian but secular, the context and method of evangelism is shifting toward that of the era before Constantine.

The Content of Evangelism in Renewing Churches

First, I believe evangelism in the renewing church is recovering the emphasis that Christ's death is a victory over the powers of evil. Christ has destroyed evil by his death and resurrection. He has dethroned principalities and spiritual powers (1 Cor. 15:24, 26); he has "disarmed principalities and powers, He made a public spectacle of them, triumphing over them" (Col. 2:15). This was a cosmic battle, a cosmic victory.

But now, in the interim between the resurrection of Christ and his coming in judgment, the church, his kingdom on earth where he now rules, is the scene of this cosmic struggle. Christ has extended to his body, his power, his authority, his victory over evil through the Holy Spirit in the church. Evangelism calls people into his kingdom, into his church, under his rule. The renewing church understands that it is enlisting the saved to participate in Christ's victory over evil, to *extend* Christ's victory to every area of life.

Second, contemporary evangelism seems to be restoring the sense that a relationship with Christ demands radical obedience. This obedience begins by demanding the full identification of the believer with Christ by baptism.

Baptism in many evangelical churches has lost its meaning. In many cases the gospel has been reduced to "something good for you." To be baptized into Christ means to identify with his suffering, to enter into his death, and to be raised to new life in him. In this way the Christian participates in the victory of Christ over evil and is called in his body, the church, to continue to wage war against evil, wherever it is found, in Christ's power and authority.

Salvation means to participate in the new era. It means to be delivered from our sin, to be called into a new way of life. This is not only in an individual sense, but also in the corporate sense of the church, which is the new creation. Bruce J. Nicholls in "The Kingdom of God, the Church and the Future of Mankind" insisted that evangelicals must begin where Jesus began—with the preaching of the kingdom. This kingdom is "the reign of God. Whenever Christ reigns there the Kingdom is manifest." But the kingdom of God is more than an eschatological hope; it is a present reality as well. It is found now in the church, among the people God has called out and together. "Both the Kingdom and the church," wrote Nicholls, "are dynamic organisms which are manifest in redeemed people. The church is both the contextualizing of the Kingdom on earth and the divinely appointed agent for spreading the Kingdom throughout the world."[7]

Third, contemporary evangelism increasingly recognizes that biblical evangelism speaks to all of human existence.

Dr. Willem Visser't Hooft in his retiring speech as general secretary of the World Council of Churches at the Uppsala Assembly in 1966 said: "A Christianity which has lost its vertical dimension has lost its salt, and is not only insipid in itself, but useless to the world. But a Christianity which would use the vertical dimension as a means of escape from responsibility for and in the common life of men is a denial of the incarnation of God's life for the world manifested in Christ."[8] This statement contains in a nutshell the essence of kingdom evangelism. The whole person in all vertical and horizontal relationships must be brought under the jurisdiction of Jesus Christ.

In summary, what is needed is a return to a kingdom evangelism that not only *announces* the kingdom but also seeks to *inaugurate* the kingdom in the biblical sense. Our evangelism must stress that obedience in the world results in the application of kingdom teaching and living in every area of life.

True obedience means that we are called to forsake the false gods of our culture. All too often we have identified false gods as personal sins only. There is no question that the Christian is called to flee the personal sins of immorality, impurity, passion, evil desires, greed, anger, wrath, malice, slander, abusive speech, lying, and the like. To live by these values is to live under the rule of Satan. But when we fail to recognize the controlling presence of these sins not only in our hearts but also in the very warp and woof of society, we miss both the depth of the biblical understanding of sin and the depth of the kingdom of God as the rule of Christ in every area of life. In other words, to reduce the rule of the kingdom to our personal experience apart from our activity in society and culture is to deny the lordship of Christ over all of life.

The Method of Evangelism in the Renewing Churches

At the time of this writing very few Protestant renewing churches are aware of local church evangelism practices in the third century. This form of evangelism is being resurrected mainly among the renewing Catholic churches.

However, there is absolutely no reason why third-century evangelism cannot be successfully adapted among renewing churches within Protestantism. And I believe it will be increasingly used as the knowledge of it spreads. It should take hold in the Protestant community for several reasons.

First, third-century evangelism is thoroughly evangelical. It preaches Christ. It calls people into the church. It demands radical obedience.

Second, third-century evangelism is *local church evangelism par excellence*. It does not bring people to Christ at mass rallies on television and turn them loose to find their way in the faith. Rather, it emanates from the local church and manifests a personal caring touch in which a person is taken by the hand and walked through the various stages of growth and development into conversion.

The community of God's people in a local church therefore plays a supportive role, not only for the person who is evangelizing but also for the person being evangelized. One is not subjected to an individualistic salvation where one stands alone but is introduced to a community of people who provide social, moral, and psychological assistance to the converting person who is undergoing a radical change in life.

Third, early church evangelism does not replace current forms of evangelism. Rather, it supplements them by providing a plan whereby converting persons can be brought into a deeper and lasting commitment to Christ and the church. Therefore, mass rallies, television evangelism, and all the various forms of one-on-one evangelism can be treated as the inquiry stage of evangelism. They may lead a person to Christ and to the door of the church where the supportive process of continuing what has begun brings depth to the initial commitment.

Finally, it ought to be noted that this kind of evangelism not only relates to the secular age in which we live but also contains elements that pertain to the changing needs of people. It is personal, visual, developmental, thoroughly related to a person's life in the world.

11
EDUCATION IN THE EARLY CHURCH

Most mission models of the recent past are based on the concept that evangelism and education are two different functions of the church. This questionable view finds support in C. H. Dodd's *The Apostolic Preaching and Its Development*. Dodd's thesis is that "It was by kerygma . . . not by didache that it pleased God to save men."[9] This loss of evangelism in education as well as the loss of education in evangelism is one of the root causes of superficiality in evangelism today. The message of Christianity is a *historical* message with *content*.

Whenever Christianity is preached without its history or content, it is reduced to a social or psychological panacea, or worse yet, a mere manipulation of feelings, moving the individual into a contentless response. On the other hand, whenever the content of Christianity is presented as factual or intellectual data without the accompanying call to commitment and change of life, Christian education loses its power to form character in the convert. Clearly, evangelism and education must stand together. There must be content in preaching and proclamation in teaching.

Although a number of scholars have questioned Dodd's conclusion, it wasn't until the publication of *Preaching and Teaching in the Earliest Church* by R. C. Worley that Dodd's conclusions were exposed by a full-scale treatment. Worley showed, as Michael Green also suggested in *Evangelism in the Early Church,* that in "both rabbinic Judaism and in early Christianity there was no such clear-cut distinction between the work of the evangelist and the teacher."[10] Paul's example at Ephesus where "he went into the synagogue and spoke boldly for three months, reasoning and persuading concerning the things of the kingdom of God" (Acts 19:8) suggests that the mission of the church to the unconverted was accompanied by a rigorous intellectual activity. We have seen the example of how education and evangelism were brought together in the evangelism model set forth by Hippolytus.

In this chapter I will stress the educational dimension of early church evangelism and life. But first allow me to mention some problems in current Christian education that this ancient model will help to correct.

PROBLEMS IN CONTEMPORARY CHRISTIAN EDUCATION

Christian educators generally agree that today's church needs to overcome three specific problems related to Christian education. They are an overemphasis on moralism, a reduction of learning to factualism, and a failure to see things holistically.

First, moralism resembles a do-goodism that neglects a more biblical understanding of Christian ethics as it grows out of the redemptive work of Christ. The moralistic teacher tends to find "the moral" in Bible stories and in the lives of biblical heroes. There is a tendency to emphasize how "doing good" and "being responsible" always pay off in the end. On this basis the teacher urges the students to be helpful, kind, and sharing. In other words moralism is sometimes substituted for moral teaching.

The problem with this kind of teaching is not with the behavior suggested by moralism, but with the context in which it is found. Sometimes moralism is a misinterpretation of what the Scripture *actually* says. Also, it fails to emphasize the redemptive nature of the Word. The stories of Scripture often are explained as isolated incidents of interest. They are not set forth as examples of the way God is working to accomplish redemption. Thus the picture of Christianity as a superficial do-goodism is unconsciously presented. For example, if we treat the story of Abraham merely as an example of obedience without putting Abraham in the context of God's covenant to bring into existence a people to his praise and his purpose, we reduce the story of Abraham to moralism.

Second, factualism is similar to moralism in that it calls for the mere memorization of material apart from an understanding of the meaning of that material. It is good for a student to know the periods of biblical history and to know what happened in each period. But unless the student knows *why* what is happening is happening, the whole point is missed. A mere memorization of the names of the kings, or of the important dates, events, places, and people of the Bible is only forgotten unless the role they play in the unfolding of the redemptive process is made clear.

What is the redemptive meaning of Seth, Abraham, Moses, David, and Jeremiah? How is God working in history to bring Christ into the world? What does God's action mean in relation to the human predicament? What am I to do about it? Unless these questions are probed— along with the teaching of facts—the education given can make no claim to be really Christian at its root because it does not shape perception and behavior.

Third, the failure to see the complete picture is similar to the failure of moralism and factualism. A Christian education without a biblical framework on which to hang what is being taught provides only scattered information, bits and pieces of truth that never come together in a whole. For this reason it is imperative to have a good grasp of the entire Christian faith. In this context education improves, deepens, and strengthens the learners' grasp of the claims Christ makes over the whole of life.

The basic problem with moralism, factualism, and the failure to see the complete picture is that they do not lend themselves to the increase of real growth in the Christian faith, to its understanding as well as living out of it. In short they do not educate and evangelize. These errors tend to support an individualistic approach to Christianity. Consequently, they provide an inadequate basis for faith, fail to further a deepening sense of commitment to Christ, and do not succeed in showing how the Christian faith relates to all of life. We turn, therefore, to the early church in search of guidelines for an agenda for education.

CHRISTIAN EDUCATION IN THE EARLY CHURCH

There are three ways we can gain information about education in the early church. First, by looking at the initial response to the message in the inquiry; second, by examining the earliest Christian catechism in the catechumenate; and third, by reviewing the content of catechetical instruction. In all these examples we will see that education in the early church was related to the various steps of evangelism.

The Inquiry

According to Hippolytus' *The Apostolic Tradition*, pre-evangelism education was practiced in Rome by the end of the second century. At this time prospective converts were organized into three groups: seekers, hearers, and kneelers. The seeker was an inquirer, the hearer one who was enrolled in the three-year catechetical class, and the kneeler was the believer who was in the final stages of instruction before baptism (six weeks before Easter; baptism was on Easter Sunday). But our concern here is with the seeker. Showing an interest in the Christian faith, this person was brought to the church for an inquiry with the leaders of the congregation. The purpose of this conference was to communicate the *demands* the Christian faith makes on its converts (like an education on the cost of discipleship).

What we learn from the comments of Hippolytus is that a person who desired to follow Jesus Christ was confronted with the implications of discipleship before being allowed to enroll in the hearers' class. For example, if a person was engaged in an occupation that involved idol worship or allegiance to the emperor as God, that job must be given up. If a person was involved in practices contrary to the gospel, such as astrology or immorality, they must be given up.

In other words, the implications of repentance are not only on inner attitudes but on outer actions as well. More than likely many people were turned away from the faith when they discovered the kind of obedience it demanded. Congregations may have been smaller as a result, but the degree of commitment may have been stronger.

But what about the content? What were these people who became hearers, in preparation for baptism and full membership into the church, taught? Fortunately, several early catechetical documents have been discovered that provide insight into the contents of evangelism-education. We know from these documents that early Christian instruction centered around orthopraxis (correct living) and orthodoxy (correct doctrine).

The Catechumenate

According to *The Apostolic Tradition*, there is a considerable period of instruction before baptism: "Let catechumens spend three years as hearers of the word. But if a man is zealous and perseveres well in the work, it is not time but his character that is decisive."[11] This period of time for instruction was called the catechumenate. We may ask: What was the converting person taught?

The preaching of the apostles always called for a response to the gospel facts. Since the initial response of preaching was for the hearer to be baptized, it is through the earliest baptismal creeds that we gain insight into the *content* of early Christian teaching. These creeds appear basic, such as, "I believe Jesus is Lord" (Rom. 10:9) or "I believe Jesus is the Christ, the Son of the living God" (Matt. 16:16; John 20:31) or the more expanded creed of Paul in 1 Corinthians 15:3–5, "that Christ died for our sins according to the Scriptures, and that He was buried, and that He rose again the third day according to the Scriptures, and that He was seen by Cephas." These early hearers of the gospel were hearing the faith, not formulating the faith.

That a deeper education in the faith and an incorporation into the new community through baptism began immediately after conversion is suggested by Acts 2:42. Here the new Christians "continued steadfastly in the apostles' doctrine and fellowship, in the breaking of bread, and in prayers." It is most natural that this pattern should develop since the Jewish synagogue was a place of instruction and worship. According to Acts 2:46, it appears that this postbaptismal instruction was on a "daily" basis. But what was the content of this instruction? To answer this question we turn to an examination of the earliest Christian catechism.

The Earliest Christian Catechism

Philip Carrington has attempted to reconstruct the early teaching of the church in his work *The Primitive Christian Catechism*. His argument is that the earliest Christian catechisms were modeled after the Jewish form of instruction. The method of teaching was through both oral and written means. The emphasis was not so much on speculative matters as it was on behavior or on "walking." He argues interestingly and effectively that the New Testament documents yield traces of this teaching that drew on the Old Testament pattern.

Jewish teaching, for example, began with Leviticus, a catechetical summary of religious duties. The central chapters of this catechism are chapters 19–20, the so-called "holiness code." And within this code two verses are of supreme importance: The first is Leviticus 19:2, "You shall be holy; for I the LORD your God am holy," and second, Leviticus 19:18, "you shall love your neighbor as yourself." These two verses constitute the key to Jewish catechetical instruction. The theme of their instruction—the holiness of God and love for neighbor—appear frequently and with some apparent organization in the New Testament literature, suggesting that parts of the New Testament are the actual material of the earliest catechetical instruction of the church. (Be holy: see Matt. 5:48; 1 Thess. 4:7; 1 Peter 1:16; 1 John 3:3. For love: see Matt. 5:43; 1 Thess. 4:9; 1 Peter 1:22; 1 John 3:10).

Correct Living

The earliest catechetical noncanonical document of the church is the *Didache*, a short sixteen-chapter document that is dated as early as A.D. 50 and as late as A.D. 130. The *Didache* begins "there are two ways, one of life, one of death; and between the two ways there is a great difference." The way of life consists of a number of instructions on how to live, drawn mainly from the teachings of Jesus, particularly his Sermon on the Mount. The "way of death," which begins in chapter 5, is a catalog of evils similar to those found in the Epistles. An interesting point about the use of "the two ways" is the thoroughly Jewish nature of the approach. Much of the material included in "the two ways" is found in Leviticus chapters 17–19. Research into the origins of "the two ways," as Lewis Sherrill pointed out in *The Rise of Christian Education*, suggests with a "high degree of probability, that this part of the *didache* was drawn by the Christian teachers from Jewish material used in the instruction of proselytes to Judaism."[12]

The idea of "the two ways" came into focus as early as the wisdom literature. Proverbs 4:18–19 refers to the "path of the righteous" and "the way of the wicked." Philip Carrington suggested that the two ways are "to be looked on as the catechetical material of the Greek synagogue designed for hearers or catechumens of all kinds, whether children or adult proselytes.[13] We know that the term "way" was used of Christianity in the New Testament as well. In Acts 19:23, the apostle Paul caused much disturbance in Ephesus through his teaching of the "way." The

Gentiles brought into the Christian faith had to be taught the fundamentals of morality and Christian behavior.

To communicate Christian morality the apostles seemed to adopt the Jewish method of "the two ways." This seems apparent in Paul's writings. In Galatians 5, Paul listed the sins that characterize those who live "according to the flesh" and the virtues that result from "walking in the spirit." In Colossians 3 he lists what the new man is to "put off" and what he is "to put on." In Romans 6 he urges converts to "yield yourselves to God" and "do not yield your members to sin." This comparison between the way of life and the way of death appears less explicitly, but nevertheless clearly, within the practical portions of all the New Testament writings.

It is no wonder then that Christians are instructed to walk in the way of life and to avoid the way of death. This would be particularly true for Gentile converts to the faith who did not have the advantage of the Jewish moral emphasis.

The evidence is that Christians coming for baptism had to attest to a good character, that indeed they did live by the way of life. Justin pointed out that only those who "promise they can live accordingly" are baptized.[14] Hippolytus wrote, "They who are to be set apart for baptism shall be chosen after their lives have been examined: whether they have lived soberly, whether they have honoured the widows, whether they have visited the sick, whether they have been active in well-doing."[15] Clearly orthopraxis was as important in the early church as orthodoxy.

Correct Practice

The second area in which the new convert had to show proof of real conversion before baptism was that of orthodoxy—right belief. Christian faith is not contentless.

163

It has to do with an inward and outward profession of the faith. "The gospel," wrote G. R. Beasley-Murray in *Baptism in the New Testament*, "lays a demand on men, to which an obedient response should be given. It calls for a man to cease from himself, to own allegiance to Christ and repose trust in Him . . . all this makes it clear that in the New Testament faith is no mere intellectual acceptance of a set of religious propositions. It has the Lord Christ as its object and calls forth a response of the whole man to Him."[16]

Paul made the content-orientation of baptism clear in Romans 6 where he indicates that the form of baptism itself speaks to the content of the Christian faith. As Christ died, was buried, and rose from the dead, so the convert who confesses Jesus confesses these facts about Christ and recognizes his identification in Jesus' act for the forgiveness of sin by himself symbolizing the death, burial, and Resurrection in baptism. It is clear, then, that to confess Christ is to acknowledge the truth of the gospel about him. The convert confesses faith in the person, but not apart from who that person is and what that person has done.

During three years of instruction the hearer was given a firm basis in the structure of Christian orthodoxy over against the teaching and practice of the heretic. And when the time for baptism came, the convert confessed Christ as he or she had been instructed. According to Hippolytus the convert "renounced Satan and all his works, then was taken to the water where the following confession was made along with the baptism":

> "Dost thou believe in God, the father almighty?" And he who is being baptized shall say:
> "I believe."
> Then holding his hand placed on his head, he shall baptize him once.

And then he shall say:

"Dost thou believe in Christ Jesus, the Son of God, who was born of the virgin Mary and was crucified under Pontius Pilate, and was dead and buried, and rose again the third day, alive from the dead, and ascended into heaven and sat at the right hand of the Father, and will come to judge the quick and the dead?" And when he says:

"I believe."

He is baptized again. And again he shall say:

"Dost thou believe in (the) Holy Ghost, and the holy church, and the resurrection of the flesh?"

He who is being baptized shall say accordingly:

"I believe",

And so is baptized a third time.[17]

During the three years of instruction preceding baptism the convert was trained in the meaning of the creed. Through this "confessional" approach to the Christian faith the convert understood what was believed, why it was believed, and how his life was to be different.

An indication of the actual content of early Christian education has been preserved for us in a number of catechetical lectures. One of the most important of these is *The Catechetical Lectures* of Cyril of Jerusalem (d. 386).

In lectures 1–3 he spoke of the temper of mind necessary for baptism. He writes of sin, the devil, repentance, remission of sin, and the meaning of baptism. In lecture 4 he spoke of the ten Christian dogmas: belief about God, Christ, the virgin birth, Christ's crucifixion and burial, the Resurrection, the Second Coming and judgment; the Holy Spirit; the Cross; and man's nature and end. He then lectured on the subject of faith, followed by thirteen lessons on the creed. Here, in a most interesting manner, is set forth the content of the Christian faith that a convert should know before baptism. We are well justified in concluding that evangelism and education in the early church were regarded in a holistic manner, not as separate functions but as the mission of the church.

EDUCATION IN THE RENEWING CHURCHES

The renewing churches that have adopted the early church method of education emphasize three special motifs. (This education is seen in relationship not only to the converting person but also to the person who has been converted and is in an active relationship to Christ and the church.) They are education related to baptism; education in the context of the church; and education that results in Christian behavior.

Education Related to Baptism

Baptism provides the context in which a person may really come to grips with the Christian faith. The heart of the Christian faith is represented in baptism. To identify with the death, burial, and resurrection of Christ; to be initiated into the power of his resurrection; to be enlisted as a soldier in the cosmic battle over evil; to participate in the church, the presence of the kingdom; to become a disciple of Christ; to obey the will of the king; to anticipate the return of Christ—all these images and more are contained within baptism.

In the third century the entire local congregation participated with the catechumens in a special six weeks of preparation before Easter. In this way they *repeated* their baptismal vows and renewed their commitment to Jesus Christ. (This may account for the origin of Lent.) The entire congregation relived their commitment to Christ's body, recalling, with the new converts, the cycle of repentance, faith, and obedience, which they re-enacted through rituals and symbols, and which enriched and strengthened the community in both orthodoxy and orthopraxis. Thus, education in the early church was not only related to baptism but also to the cycle of events in the church year that led up to baptism.

What is happening in the renewing churches today, particularly in Catholic congregations that have restored liturgical evangelism, is an education revolving around the church year that sees baptism as a symbol of a relationship with Christ toward which the church moves (as in Advent, Christmas, Epiphany, Lent) and the symbol from which the church proceeds (as in Pentecost and Trinity seasons). Since baptism symbolizes both orthodoxy and orthopraxis, the full content of the Christian message can be organized into the educational mission of the church in the various periods of the church year.

For example, an Advent study can emphasize the Old Testament prophecies regarding the coming of Christ; an Epiphany study can stress the Judean ministry of Jesus when he first manifested himself as the Son of God; a Lenten study can emphasize the teachings of Jesus about himself and the meaning of his life and impending death; a Pentecost study can concentrate on the early church in Acts 1–15; and classes during Trinity season can probe the missionary advance of the early church and the development of its literature. In this way the whole program of education moves with the life of Christ, from the prophecies of his coming to his death and resurrection at Easter (the most appropriate time for baptism). After Easter, education and growth in Christ are defined by Pentecost and the spread of the church.

Education in the Context of the Church

The kind of education explained above is a corporate education that occurs within the church as a community. The spiritual journey coincides not only with the life of Christ and the early church but also with *each other*.

There is the growing awareness that Christian nurture must happen in a dynamic, integral, and transactional way within the church as the body of Christ. In this context orthodoxy and orthopraxis are being brought together in the relational way in which they were originally understood and practiced.

In *A Theology of Christian Education* Larry Richards recognized and argued for an education that takes place within the church, based on new life. Richards argued that conversion brings the believer out of death into new life. But this new life is not to be thought of individualistically nor in the static sense. It is life in the body, and a life of continual growth. He wrote:

> Christian education then can never deal with individual life alone. Christian education has to concern itself with the processes within the Body which nurture corporate and individual growth in Christ. Any Christian educational approach which focuses on either the individual or the group in exclusion of the other is bound to fall short.[18]

This life orientation of education forces us to recognize the place of the church in the life of the believer. Christians are not an "entity unto themselves." If there is one thing, among others, that the biblical concept of the church teaches us, it is that the church is to be seen as a whole. To be in Christ means to be in the church. If the whole church is present in every local congregation, then education cannot be divorced from the life of the whole church. The entire congregation together seeks to become Christlike. It is in this context of the goal of the whole body that education must take place.

Furthermore, the discovery that orthodox belief and orthodox living are not to be separated, but constitute the two sides of a single piece, makes it clear that growth in these two aspects can take place only in the church. It is the church that has received the faith of the apostles.

The church preserves it and passes it on, not just in creeds but also in living. Consequently, growth takes place in a transactional relationship. The church models the truth, it incarnates the truth, it has "this mind in you which was in Christ Jesus." Therefore, Christians are to be nurtured in the context of the church. The church as a body is to mature and become more Christlike.

The dynamic that causes this Christlikeness to happen is love. Religious education, both in the Hebrew and Christian past, had to do with life; its motivating force then as now was love. As we have seen, both the holiness code and the early catechetical teaching of the church were modeled on love toward God and love toward other persons. This brought together both content and action. The content of orthodoxy was "as I have loved you" and the practice of orthopraxis was so "you also love one another" (John 13:14).

As the church corporately knows and loves God, so its members corporately know and love one another. In this context education is not mere moralism, a bare fact, or a partial insight, but a holistic experience of learning to love God and fellow persons in the context of a loving community. Theory and experience are realized in living!

Education in the Context of Behavior

The new developments in Christian education pioneered by Ted Ward and Donald Joy, which are based on the research of Jean Piaget and Lawrence Kohlberg, are making an impact on Christian education.

Because the views of Piaget and Kohlberg are based on highly complex and detailed views of man that some educators regard as consistent with the biblical views of man as well as the biblical perspective of growth through nurture, I will concentrate on a summary of their main emphases. The Piaget-Kohlberg findings as they relate to Christian education may be summarized as follows:

1. A holistic view of man. Because each aspect of the human person is interrelated with the other, facts and feelings are learned together.
2. A positive view of man. Development is a natural process of humans. Each person has the potential to reach a high level of development. This is true in both the cognitive and moral aspects of persons.
3. Man is active. Human beings are born to mature. Concepts gradually form in the person. When initial immature concepts conflict with other concepts a process of equilibration occurs, and gradually interpretations are formed.
4. Man in transaction. Maturation occurs through transactions with the physical world and with social interaction. Through this process people become increasingly aware of possible interpretations other than their own.

The implications of this theory of development appear obvious for evangelism and Christian education. The essence of evangelism and education is to bring a person into the Christian perception of reality, to see growth and maturation within the church as a nurturing community where transactions between growing persons are continually taking place in the context of faith and of works.

There are numerous applications of this theory that are now beginning to make their way into the curriculum of the churches. Some of the basic applications are:

1. The conviction that the church must be seen as a transactional context in which growth takes place.

The impersonal church where people meet once or twice or more a week must give way to the more personal community-centered church. In this context people become caringly involved with each other, experiencing what it means to be the body of Christ.

2. The new convert to Christianity must be brought into the church community immediately. The convert has been born into a new family, and it is in this family that the new Christian is nurtured and brought into a mature Christian faith. In this context three of the four causes for growth occur: 1) direct experience; 2) social interaction; and 3) equilibration. Bumping shoulders with more mature Christians and finding models who provide examples for growth take place within the church community.

3. Consequently, the church must be accepting of new Christians and provide a context of warmth and love in which the new convert is given the freedom to question, experiment, and grow.

I have argued that Christian education is not a mere memorization of facts, nor a moralization of Scripture. Instead the early church and now the renewing church recognize that the goal of Christian education is to bring together orthodoxy and orthopraxis in the life of the church and in the life of each individual in the church.

Education cannot be divorced from the life context of the church. Evangelism brings us into the church, into Christ's body, where, through our association with Christian truth in the living context of our relationship to other members of Christ's body, we are to grow. Thus, the church is the context through which both our understanding and our practice of Christianity are nurtured. Christian education is therefore not the gaining of a mere abstract knowledge, but the assimilation of a new lifestyle, characterized by a new perception of reality and a living that conforms to the values of the Christian community.

12
SOCIAL ACTION IN THE EARLY CHURCH

The third aspect of the mission of the church is to *apply the work of Christ to the world as a way of witnessing to the ultimate recapitulation of all things in the new heavens and the new earth*. In evangelism and education the work of Christ forms the church, the society within the society. In social action the people who have been formed after the image of Christ in the church influence the world and witness to the application of the work of Christ to the entire creation—to nature and to the structures of life, such as the family, government, education, and business.

A PROBLEM IN CONTEMPORARY THOUGHT

There are some who ignore the larger mission of the church, treating the relationship of the church to society and to culture with a degree of indifference.

A basic reason for indifference toward society and culture may be found in the failure to recognize the world-view nature of the Christian faith as well as in a minimized view of the battle which the Christian world-view must wage with the powers of evil.

For example, the failure to affirm the doctrine of creation results in an inability to come to grips with history and the meaningfulness of life; the privatization of sin results in an ignoring of the permeation of sin in all the structures of society and in the works of culture; the spiritualization of the Incarnation prevents a wrestling with the event of Christ as the inauguration of a new beginning in history; and an individualized view of the church stands in the way of understanding what it means to be the new creation in the midst of the old.

There are several unfortunate results of this failure to come to grips with a biblical world-view. The first is the split created between the so-called secular and sacred aspects of life: the view that implies that those acts that are spiritual are sacred and those activities that are natural and physical are secular. Therefore it is sacred to pray, to read the Bible, to witness, and to go to church. But work, play, and cultural activities are secular.

This dichotomy is an "other-worldly," "this worldly" conflict. It fosters a superspirituality, a private ethic, a Christianity that can successfully withdraw from the conflicts of the world. It causes one to live as though a dichotomy exists between spirit and matter, sacred and secular. It supports loving God with the "heart," but shrinks from loving him by actions in the social order, or in the public aspects of life.

Piety becomes exclusively private—something practiced at home, in the quiet time, at church, or in the private decisions of life.

The second result of the failure to have a biblical world-view is a retreat from the cosmic battle in which the church is really engaged. Because Christ's death is cosmic—having to do with the whole of creation—the battle in which the church is now engaged in the period between Pentecost and the Second Coming must be one that *recalls* Christ's victory over sin through the Resurrection and *anticipates* the consummation of his victory over evil in his return. This means that, although evil permeates every area of life, the hope of the church is the reign of Christ in all of life; and the task of the church is to realize that reign in life now—as much as possible.

THE MISSION OF THE CHURCH TO THE WORLD IN THE EARLY CHURCH

While there is a considerable amount of commentary in the early Fathers on Christians and how they should relate to the world, none summarized it better than the anonymous author of the second-century document, *Epistle to Diognetus:*

> For Christians cannot be distinguished from the rest of the human race by country or language or customs. They do not live in cities of their own; they do not use a peculiar form of speech; they do not follow an eccentric manner of life. . . . [they] follow the customs of the country in clothing and food and other matters of daily living. . . . They marry, like everyone else, and they beget children, but they do not cast out their offspring. They share their board with each other, but not their marriage bed. It is true that they are "in the flesh," but they do not live "according to the flesh." They busy themselves on earth, but their citizenship is in heaven. . . . To put it simply: What the soul is in the body, that Christians are in the world.[19]

The essential teaching of the early church regarding how Christians live in the world is captured in the threefold tension expressed in the epistle: (1) the church is separated from the world; (2) the church is nevertheless identified with the world; and (3) the church seeks to transform the world.

The Church Is Separated from the World

The concept of separation is rooted in those Scriptures that stress the otherworldliness of the Christian life. Its Christ-model is the crucified Lord, the suffering servant, the one whose power is in the weakness of the cross. Its ethos is that of a people who are "strangers and pilgrims in an alien land," a people who believe they are not to "love the world or the things of the world," a people who do good to all men but "especially those who are of the household of faith," a people who firmly believe that it is possible and indeed necessary to live by the Sermon on the Mount. Its patron saint is Peter who reminds them that they are "a chosen race, a royal priesthood, a holy nation, God's own people."

For all this Christians expect to suffer, to be misunderstood, to be reviled, to be persecuted for righteousness' sake. But that is not of ultimate importance because separationalists look to a city "whose builder and maker is God." Furthermore, seeing that "all these things are to be dissolved" they concern themselves with "what sort of persons they ought to be in lives of holiness and godliness."

One of the earliest Christian thinkers to espouse the separational model was Tertullian, the great third-century theologian of North Africa. In his pre-Constantinian world, paganism permeated all of life. Consequently, Tertullian admonished Christians to shun much of life—to refrain from involvement in politics, military service, and trade and business. He even regarded literature, theater, and music as ministers of sin. For our interest, the most important principle to derive from Tertullian is his belief that Christianity is antiestablishment, and that it contains the seeds of a countercultural movement. Christianity stands *against the powers of evil wherever they may be found*. Therefore the Christian, as the *Epistle to Diognetus* states, does not participate in the evil in society.

The Church Is Identified with the World

The concept of identification stands in the tradition of Scripture that stresses the this-worldliness character of the Christian faith. Its Christ-model is the incarnate Lord, the one who through living in the world can identify with the struggles and tensions of life. Its ethos revolves around the Jesus who ate and drank with the "tax collectors and sinners," with the tension of Paul who, when he wanted to do right found that "evil lies close at hand." Its concern is to affirm the abundant life declared by Jesus and recognized by Paul who insisted that "all things are lawful." It wishes to "render unto Caesar those things that are Caesar's," to uphold the state, to pray for kings and emperors, and to admonish slaves and servants to be obedient to their masters.

The *Epistle to Diognetus* clearly states that the Christian is not a revolutionary attempting to overthrow the governments of the world and to establish the kingdom of God by force. Christians participate in the life of the world, in its works, play, and customs of speech and dress.

The Church Seeks to Transform the World

The transformationalist stands in the tradition of those Scriptures that emphasize the power of the gospel to change not only the life of an individual but also the life of culture. Its Christ-model is the resurrected Christ who reigns in power and glory over the entire cosmos. Its ethos is based on the assertion that God was pleased to dwell in Christ "and by Him to reconcile all things to Himself, whether things on earth or things in heaven, having made peace through the blood of His cross" (Col. 1:20). Its vision is like that of the prophets who demanded, "let justice run down like water, and righteousness like a mighty stream" (Amos 5:24). Like Isaiah it sees that "heaven is

My throne, and earth is My footstool. Where is the house that you would build Me? And where is the place of My rest? For all those things My hand has made, And all those things exist, says the LORD" (Isa. 66:1–2). The Christian's responsibility on earth is to witness the transformation of the world so "Your will be done, on earth as it is in heaven" (Matt. 6:10) may become a reality.

One of the earliest figures to espouse the transformational model was Augustine who, in his vision of society, saw two cities existing side by side, the city of man under a secular rule and the city of God under a sacred rule. Augustine saw Christ as the transformer of culture, as the one who redirects and regenerates the unfolding of culture. Augustine did not accept what is as what ought to be. He saw what is as a result of a corrupt and perverse nature. This result of sin was everywhere—in human nature and in the social sinfulness of mankind. But Christ, Augustine argued, had come to convert and redirect humanity, who, in turn, should influence culture to redirect, reshape, and transform the world to the glory of God. The author of the *Epistle to Diognetus* captured this sense in the statement, "What the soul is in the body, that Christians are in the world."

SOCIAL ACTION IN THE RENEWING CHURCH TODAY

In my opinion, this threefold tension between church and world defines the emerging consensus on the church today.

First, the renewing church recognizes the existence and work of the powers of evil in the world. Therefore, it calls for a separation from these powers. A new interest in the presence of powers acting through the structures of existence has caused renewalists to recognize the validity of a church that takes a stand against the ruling powers. For example, churches are urging members not to work in abortion clinics nor to be involved in the manufacture of nuclear warheads.

Because the Christian is redeemed and is called to live both personally and communally by a new set of standards, the believer is called to be separate from the powers that rule this world. The gods of materialism, sensualism, greed, war, hate, oppression, and injustice are no longer to rule the Christian. Renewing churches believe that the Christian belongs to a new community and, as a new being, is responsible to live by the standards of the kingdom. Thus, the people of the renewing church are increasingly willing to take a stand against the evils perpetrated through the structures of society. A refusal to support directly or indirectly abortion, apartheid, pornography, drugs and alcoholism, oppression and injustice, materialism and consumerism is one way in which the renewing church can express its stand against the evils of our age.

Second, the renewing church also recognizes the need to identify with the structures of existence. There seems to be a new sense that this is not Satan's world. It is God's, and, as such, it is the arena in which the Christian's redemptive activity takes place. While the renewing church recognizes the sinful nature of humanity, it does not commit the error of identifying sin with physical nature or creatureliness. Therefore, like the people of the early church, renewalists do not differ in the basic customs of the general culture. They marry, bring children into the world, pursue education, work in industry, banking, health care, and the like. They are not "odd men out." They are normal, life-pursuing people.

Yet, the third point is, the renewing church acknowledges the validity of seeking to transform the world. It affirms the new order in the midst of the old, calling the old into a repentance and a turning away from the spirit of the

Antichrist toward a renewal effected by the cosmic redemption of Christ. The renewing church recognizes that redeemed persons are to influence their culture and may by their witness cause change in a given situation. Such a witness may result in more equitable economic patterns, more just laws, and less oppression and dehumanization.

Those who believe in renewal, it may be said, are sensitive to their calling to be "salt" and "light" to the world. They want to witness not only privately but also publicly through their lives and the values they express in every situation.

Therefore, the renewing church is developing a model of the relationship between the church and the world rooted in the example of Christ. On the one hand, like Christ, renewalists want to identify with the world, speak prophetically to the world, and minister to the world in a priestly fashion. On the other hand, the renewing church recognizes that Jesus is lord over all systems, ideologies, and institutions. Thus, the confession, "Jesus is Lord," looks to the day when Christ will have put all evil away forever, the day when swords will be turned into plowshares, the day when the lion and the lamb will lie down together.

Consequently, the work of the church in the world, as in the early church, is done with the ultimate vision of a restored universe in mind. The result is a new kind of activism motivated not only by *Christus Victor* but also by the vision of recapitulation of all things in the new heavens and the new earth.

Conclusion

I began this chapter by recalling the church and the barn in the mission compound where my parents served Christ in Africa. These two buildings symbolize, I suggested, the mission of the church, which is to evangelize, to educate, and to transform the world. In the renewing church today the sense of this threefold mission has not changed. What has shifted, though, from the former generation to this one, is the conviction that the mission of the church is to be done, not by individuals alone but by the work of the corporate church.

Therefore, it is my belief that what we can expect to see in the future is this: In evangelism there will be an increasing shift away from mass rallies to evangelism by the local church. Believers will bring friends and neighbors to the church, where through inquiry and instruction people will be brought into the church through conversion and baptism. The process of evangelism will be carried along through worship and education ordered by the church year and the content of the gospel proclaimed through Advent, Christmas, Epiphany, Lent, Holy Week, Easter and Pentecost.

Next, I believe that education will find a better balance, emphasizing both information and formation; again, the formation of character and development of a Christian style of life will be ordered by the events of the church year as the church year takes on the character of a personal and corporate spiritual pilgrimage.

Finally, the renewing church will increasingly play a prophetic and priestly ministry in society. Believing that the gospel applies to every area of personal, social, moral, and national life, it will seek to exert an influence on society through its presence within society. While some churches may become politicized in the process (align the church in support of a particular political ideology), most will not. Most churches will recognize that the vision out of which they live is the gospel story. Such a vision will keep the church free of particular political agendas so that it may speak to and serve the whole society.

Consequently, we will see around the world a church that is increasingly united through the sense of its task. What motivates this renewing church in this mission is the vision of a restored and re-created world. Because the church is the beginning again of this new creation, and because worship celebrates the new creation while spirituality seeks to live it out, the mission of the church is not, nor can it be, fulfilled apart from its relationship to the whole. Thus, the sense of competition between the churches in their tasks of evangelism, education, and social action will decrease in proportion to their realization that there is only one Christ, one church, and one task.

*Get the Apostolic epistles for your constant
teachers . . . dive into them as into a chest of
medicines . . . keep them in your mind.*

ST. JOHN CHRYSOSTOM, A.D. 380

*All possible care must be taken, that we
hold that faith which has been believed
everywhere, always, by all.*

VINCENT OF LÉRINS, A.D. 450

SECTION VI

The Tradition about Authority

The Tradition about Authority

I live in Wheaton, Illinois, a place that many people jokingly call "the evangelical Vatican." The presence of Wheaton College with its large administration, faculty, and staff as well as the presence here of numerous Christian organizations such as *Christianity Today*, Tyndale Publishers, and the headquarters of the Conservative Baptist denomination means that there is a decided Christian influence in this town.

It's nearly impossible to sit in a local restaurant without overhearing a conversation about the church or to shop locally without bumping into a fellow Christian or to drive a few blocks without passing a church. Christians are in every area of life here—doctors, dentists, lawyers, artists, grocers, store managers, and laborers.

For example, my dentist is a Christian. Recently, I was sitting in his dental chair with my mouth packed with the usual equipment while he drilled away at a tooth in need of attention. As usual, he was carrying on a monologue with me, a monologue that I desperately wanted to turn into a dialogue. But under the circumstances I could do nothing other than grunt a few incoherent sounds, wag my head, or flutter my eyes.

Usually, such a situation doesn't matter because the subject of the monologue isn't dealing with ultimate realities. But on this occasion my dentist was giving his opinion about theology and theologians, an opinion that is probably shared by many.

"Well, Bob," my dentist said, "I'll tell you something about you guys who teach Bible and theology." My ears pricked up, wondering what he was going to say. "I don't think you have any better understanding of truth than I do," he blurted out. Since I couldn't respond, I sat helplessly silent as he continued, "You fellows learn all that Greek and Hebrew; you study the background to the Old and New Testaments; you read all that theology; but I tell you that I think I know just as much as you do. I pick up the English text of the Bible and God reveals the same truth to me directly."

Unfortunately, I'm one of those persons who come up with a great response about two hours after the fact. So, after my dentist was finished with his discourse on theology and my tooth was restored, I politely paid my bill and left. But I kept thinking about what he said. My thoughts shifted back and forth between amusement and the urge to give him an appropriate response. Finally the answer came.

I wish I had said to him, "Well, I quite agree with you. God indeed reveals the truth to all of us. Now, why don't you sit in your chair and hand me your drill. I don't need an education in dentistry, I'll just let the Lord guide my hand and tell me what to do. I'm sure your teeth will be fine. I can do dentistry just as well as you can, so long as I depend on God."

Of course the analogy breaks down a bit, because all Christians are, in a sense, armchair theologians, while not all people are armchair dentists. Nevertheless, the point is clear. I wouldn't dare do dentistry, because I have neither an education nor a skill in that area. In other words I have no authority in that field.

Authority is a major question in every field of human thought and work. We depend on authorities not only in dentistry and the medical profession in general but also in science, technology, foreign affairs, and many other spheres of life.

The question of authority is a real issue in Christian thought as well. By what authority do we believe in *Christus Victor* and the recapitulation of the world? By what authority do we believe the church to be an extension of Christ or believe worship to be a celebration of Christ or believe spirituality to be a living out of *Christus Victor*? By what authority do we believe it to be our mission to apply that event to people and the world through evangelism, education, and social action?

Because this is such an important issue, I want to close this book with a discussion of the development of authority in the early church. I also want to show how the ancient understanding of authority is enriching the renewing church.

13
THE AUTHORITATIVE SOURCE

We face a difficult problem in putting ourselves back into the position of faith before it was well formulated. Because we live on this side of theological formulation, we have the advantage of the cumulative thought of almost two thousand years. However, if we are to succeed in grasping truth as the early church did, we may have to regard our two thousand years of cumulative theology, and especially our current position, as a disadvantage.

In a manner of reflective analysis and self-criticism we may have to suspend our theological presuppositions, denominational teachings, and personal bias in order to stand with the earliest Christians who stood on the other side of theological debate and formulation.

I frequently face this problem with my students. I tell them, "You have to step out of your twentieth-century shoes and put yourselves into the shoes of a Christian in A.D. 30. In the third decade of the first century Christians didn't have a Bible, they didn't have a creed, and they didn't have a Luther or Calvin."

Today, with the numerous translations of Scripture available, it is difficult to imagine a time when there was no New Testament canon. Nevertheless, the church existed for decades before the New Testament documents were written and for several centuries before the New Testament was organized into the present canon of Scripture.

The earliest authorities in the church were the apostles. Christians gathered around their teachings (Acts 2:42) and treated their interpretations of the tradition as authoritative (2 Thess. 2:15). Paul, who received his teachings by way of revelation (Gal. 1:12), passed his teachings on to the church (1 Cor. 15:1–4) and in particular entrusted faithful teachers to hand them over to the next generation (2 Tim. 2:2). This process of handing down the truth about Jesus Christ, his life, teachings, work, and coming again is known as apostolic tradition and apostolic succession. The tradition is the content; the succession is the means of handing the tradition down in the life of the church.

Initially apostolic teaching was handed down in the oral traditions of preaching and worship. The book of Acts, for example, contains several sermons of the apostles, such as Peter's sermon at Pentecost (Acts 2). The Epistles contain early Christian hymns (Phil. 2:5–11), catechetical materials (Gal. 5:16–26), creeds (Rom. 10:9), doxologies (Rom. 11:36), and benedictions (1 Cor. 16:23). All these materials were in existence in the oral traditions and possibly the written traditions that predate the New Testament writings.

As time went on the apostles and other church leaders included these sources in gospels and letters to meet specific needs in the Christian community. These letters and gospels were initially read to the churches when they gathered together in worship. The letters that bore the stamp of the apostles endured and those that did not, while still considered important, were relegated to a secondary status.

But it was not until the late second-century controversy with Marcion, a Gnostic, that the church began to collect the apostolic writings into an authoritative source of Christian teaching about Jesus.

THE SOURCE OF AUTHORITY IN THE EARLY CHURCH

As vicious attacks were made against apostolic Christianity, the second century proved a decisive period for the early church. These attacks, far from destroying or even modifying the faith, provided the church with a situation in which the apostolic faith was able to emerge in a clear-cut fashion, both as to its substance and its authority.

The conflict of the church with Marcion resulted in a clear understanding of the authoritative source of truth. Although Marcion, who came to Rome about A.D. 140, was influenced by Gnosticism, it is not entirely correct to call him a Gnostic. He rejected the basic Gnostic myths about the aeons that had supposedly come forth from an original divine being. But he accepted the Gnostic premise that the Old Testament was the product of an inferior God.

Irenaeus informs us that Marcion accepted the teaching of Cerdo, a Gnostic whose chief doctrine was that "the God proclaimed by the law and the prophets was not the

Father of our Lord Jesus Christ."[1] For this reason Marcion wanted to rid the church of any connection with the Old Testament or Jewish practices. The issue Marcion raised was simply this: Did the Old Testament belong to the Christian tradition?

The answer to that question was determined by the tradition that had already been set by the apostles. The apostles understood the Jewish past in terms of Christ's coming. This is evident in their attitude toward the Old Testament. They regarded the law and the prophets as well as the events and worship of Israel as part of the Christian tradition because they believed them to testify to Jesus Christ. Paul, for example, in 1 Corinthians 15:3-4, insisted that everything regarding Christ took place "according to the Scriptures."

Soon, a typological interpretation of the Old Testament as reflected in Hebrews became a standard way of interpreting Jewish Scriptures in the church. This is evident in the so-called *Epistle of Barnabas,* a treatise written around A.D. 135 in Alexandria, Egypt, in which the author wrote: "The prophets, having obtained grace from Him, prophesied concerning Him."[2] In the *Homily on the Passover* by Melito of Sardis written around A.D. 170, Melito's explanation of the paschal lamb in Exodus 12 is that it typologically points to Christ, the true Paschal Lamb.[3] And Justin Martyr in his *Dialogue with Trypho the Jew* argued that the entire Old Testament points to Jesus Christ. Therefore, the Old Testament Scriptures were regarded as the Scriptures of the New Testament church because the apostles had received this precedent from Jesus.

Marcion's opposition to the Old Testament and his concern that the writings of the apostles, which were already read widely in the church and regarded as the authoritative voice of apostolic Christianity, were entirely too Jewish led him to the formation of his own canon. He took the Gospel of Luke and the epistles of Paul, with the exception of those written to Timothy and Titus, and edited out everything that came from the Old Testament. As Irenaeus wrote:

> He dismembered the Epistles of Paul, removing all that is said by the apostle respecting that God who made the world, to the effect that he is the Father of our Lord Jesus Christ, and also those passages from the prophetical writings which the apostle quotes, in order to teach us that they announced beforehand the coming of the Lord.[4]

The reason for this drastic action on the part of Marcion is found in his interpretation of Paul's doctrine of grace. He was convinced that Paul's doctrine of grace stood in absolute antithesis to the Old Testament. He saw the Old Testament God as just, vengeful, and demanding. Salvation in the Old Testament was by law, keeping the commands, and doing good. But the New Testament God was loving and kind, practicing mercy and forgiveness, giving salvation in Christ, and making no demands.

Consequently, Marcion would have nothing to do with the Old Testament. For him, it represented another God, another salvation, another way of life. His conviction was that if Christianity continued to mix with the doctrines of this inferior religion, it would lose its distinctiveness.

Marcion's attitude toward the Old Testament and his abuse of the apostolic writings created a crucial situation for the young church. For one thing the apostles themselves had already set a precedent by interpreting the Old Testament through the death and resurrection of Christ. Were they right? The second-century church had already received the writings of the apostles as authoritative. Was the church right in doing so?

As a result of these issues, the young church was forced to decide the *authoritative source* of Christian teaching. Before the end of the second century the church affirmed the Old Testament, the four Gospels, and the letters of Paul as authoritative in their entirety. (The canonicity of some of the Catholic Epistles and the Book of Revelation remained controversial for some time.)

Even though the canon was not officially ratified by a church council until the second half of the fourth century, the church had made a decisive step toward establishing a norm for doctrine and order by the end of the second century. The authoritative norm for Christian faith and practice was the apostolic testimony to the Old Testament and the apostolic writings. In this way the church continued to stand in the tradition of Paul who had entrusted the gospel to Timothy and commanded him to pass it on to other faithful people.

Marcion's rejection of the Old Testament as well as his selective use of apostolic writings put him and his group outside the church. Although Marcionism continued with some following for a time, it gradually disappeared. After the seventh century it is heard of no more. In the meantime, the church in the middle of the second century made it clear that she had an authoritative norm for Christian teaching—the apostles—which meant that both the Old Testament and the apostolic writings were the authoritative source for Christian truth.

The reason the New Testament is so important for us today is that it was written by the apostles who give us an authoritative interpretation of the living, dying, and rising from the dead of Jesus. For example, Clement, the Bishop of Rome in A.D. 96, wrote: "The Apostles have preached the gospel to us from the Lord Jesus Christ; Jesus Christ (has done so) from God. Christ therefore was sent forth by God and the Apostles by Christ."[5]

Irenaeus tells us that Polycarp "always taught the things

which he had learned from the Apostles, which the church has handed down, and which alone are true."[6]

H. E. W. Turner in *The Pattern of Christian Truth* has successfully demonstrated the reverence of the Fathers toward holy Scripture. They were not, as Adolf Harnack once suggested, metaphysical theologians, but biblical theologians. Any reading of Justin Martyr, Irenaeus, Tertullian, Clement, Origen, Athanasius, Basil, Jerome, or Augustine shows that they are steeped in the Scriptures and that they would agree with the judgment of Saint John Chrysostom:

> Tarry not, I entreat, for another to teach thee; thou hast the oracles of God. No man teacheth thee as they; for he indeed oft grudgeth much for vainglory's sake and envy. Hearken, I entreat you, all ye that are careful for this life, and procure books that will be medicines for the soul. If ye will not any other, yet get you at least the New Testament, the *Apostolic Epistles*, [italics mine] the Acts, the Gospels, for your constant teachers. If grief befall thee, dive into them as into a chest of medicines; take thence comfort of thy trouble, be it loss, or death, or bereavement of relations; or rather dive not into them merely, but take them wholly to thee; keep them in thy mind."[7]

THE RENEWING CHURCH TODAY

Throughout this book I have attempted to demonstrate that the tapestry of faith begins with Christ and his work. I have tried to make it clear that what we trust in for our salvation is Christ. Christ, the Word, became incarnate, died, and rose again to destroy the power of the evil one and to renew the world.

In some circles, faith in Christ appears to be replaced by faith in the Bible. To make this point I sometimes say to my students, "You would think the Bible became incarnate, was crucified, and rose again for our salvation." By that statement I do not intend to demean the Bible. Instead I want to put the Bible in its proper place. It is not the object of our faith or belief. We do not believe in the Bible for our salvation. We believe in Christ. The Bible delivers Christ.

In the renewing churches I find a healthy attitude toward the Bible. I find a strong attachment to the Bible as the *source* of truth but not the *object* of truth. This view of the Bible is very similar to Luther's comment about the early Fathers. Their importance, he reminds us, is that they take us to Scripture. In similar fashion we may say that the importance of the Scripture is that it takes us to Christ.

A second feature of renewing churches is the growing awareness that the Bible belongs to the church. The church preceded the New Testament in time. Therefore, the writings of the apostles were writings in the context of the church. So the Scripture is the tradition of the church, the possession of the church. As such, the church is responsible to guard it, preserve it, pass it down, and interpret it. A major result of recognizing the Scripture as the possession of the church is the conviction that we must rediscover the church's understanding of truth.

This rediscovery of the corporate interpretation of the Scripture is a major challenge to individualistic interpretations of Christianity. The renewing church is being called to rediscover the early church's summary of the substance of faith as well as its cautionary approach to systems about the truth. We will take these matters up in the next two chapters.

14
THE AUTHORITATIVE SUBSTANCE

Christians have always been characterized by a desire to write brief summary statements of truth. In the earliest decades of the church short statements intending to summarize the context of Christian truth soon emerged. The shortest and perhaps the oldest creedal statement is "Jesus is Lord" (Rom. 10:9). Another more lengthy summary of Christian content is "Christ died for our sin according to the scriptures, he was buried, he was raised the third day" (1 Cor. 15:3–4 NIV). These statements of faith arose out of the proclamation of the gospel.

The Substance of Truth in the Early Church

Michael Green in *Evangelism in the Early Church* has discussed the content of Christian belief in relation to three terms: good news *(evangelizomai)*, to tell good news *(kerusso)*, and to bear witness *(martureo)*. He pointed out that the "good news" that Jesus proclaimed and embodied was nothing less than *the dawning of a new age*. It was introduced by the forerunner, John the Baptist, announced by Jesus at Nazareth in his reading of Isaiah 61, and preached by the disciples who declared "one subject and one only, Jesus."[8]

The central focus of this message was the redemptive death of Jesus, a death which the apostles said was for the whole world, although effective only for those who repented, believed, and followed Jesus.

The second word, to tell good news, means "to proclaim like a herald," and has reference to the same content as the "good news." In writers as varied as Matthew,

Mark, Luke, and Paul, the good news preached is "the announcement of the climax of history, the divine intervention into the affirmations of men brought about by the incarnation, life, death, resurrection and heavenly session of Jesus of Nazareth."[9] Green has also shown that the third word, "witness," which ordinarily means to attest facts or assert truths, also has reference to the same content. In Luke 24:48 Jesus commissions his disciples to be witnesses "of these things." As Green noted, these things include "the identification of Jesus as the Messiah, the fulfillment of all the scriptures in him, his suffering and death, his resurrection, and the proclamation of repentance and faith in his name to all nations, beginning from Jerusalem."[10]

The content of this apostolic preaching was soon challenged by those who would add to it as the Judaizers did, and those who would modify it as the syncretists did. For these reasons, Paul charged Timothy to "follow the pattern of the sound words which you have heard from me" and to "guard the truth that has been entrusted to you" (2 Tim. 1:13–14 RSV). Here, as John Stott commented in *Guard the Gospel*, "Paul is commanding Timothy to keep before him as his standard of sound words, or as a 'model of sound teaching' what he had heard from the Apostles."[11] Timothy is not only to *guard* the gospel but also to *pass it on*: "What you have heard from me before many witnesses entrust to faithful men who will be able to teach others also" (2 Tim. 2:2 RSV). In these passages Stott saw a fourfold progression in guarding and passing on the faith:

> First, the faith has been entrusted to Paul by Christ. . . . Secondly, what has been entrusted to Paul by Christ Paul in turn has entrusted to Timothy. . . . Thirdly, what Timothy has heard from Paul he is now to "entrust to faithful

men." . . . Fourthly, such men must be the sort of men who "will be able to teach others also."[12]

What we may see from this brief inquiry into the New Testament content of Christian truth is that the faith of the church, from the earliest times, has been characterized by a *specific content*. It is a recognizable body of truth. What was true in the New Testament period was equally true in the second century.

The picture of the church at the end of the second century is that of a number of churches (clustered around the major cities of Rome, Carthage, Alexandria, Jerusalem, and Antioch) united under their bishops, similar in worship, and grounded in the teachings of the apostles as summarized in the "rule of faith." Hegesippus, a church historian of the second century, wrote in his "Memoirs," a portion of which is still preserved in Eusebius' *Ecclesiastical History,* that he made a trip from Jerusalem to Rome and found, "In every succession . . . and in every city, the doctrine prevails according to what is declared by the law and the prophets and the Lord."[13]

The doctrine which Hegesippus referred to was not a theology, not theoretical thought, and not something that was the private possession of a few scholars. Instead his reference was to the contents of apostolic preaching, to the rule of faith, to the summary of Christian teaching that had been passed down from the apostles.

This summary of the Christian faith which emerged with clarity in the second century is not theology but what we can aptly term "a biblical framework of thought." That is to say, the contents of biblical or historic Christianity set forth the necessary presuppositions from which Christian thinking proceeds. Consequently, the content of the rule of faith was not the result of Christian thinking; rather, it was a summary of revelation: the apostles had summarized the data of revelation and passed it on. This "biblical framework" defined the perimeters within which the Christian church did her thinking.

The Origin of the Rule of Faith

Because the development of Gnosticism was such a major challenge for the second-century church, the church clarified her understanding of the *substance* of the historic faith. Christianity had already begun to be tested in the New Testament period by Judaism and esoteric religious ideas from Egypt and Persia. But the acid test of the substance of her faith came, however, when the Gnostics began to claim to have a superior knowledge handed down in a secret tradition. This knowledge, while it varied somewhat from sect to sect, basically taught the existence of two Gods—one the Spirit God who was responsible for the good, the other the Creator God (often identified with Yahweh in the Old Testament) responsible for evil.

Because the evil God was the creator, matter was regarded as evil. Naturally then, man's body, which was a product of evil, was looked upon as the prison of his soul. Salvation, then, was the release of the soul from the body so it could ultimately unite with the good Spirit God. To accomplish this, the good God sent Christ, an emanation, to bring knowledge (gnosis) that would free the soul from the body. This knowledge, which Christ gave to the disciples, the Gnostics declared, was what one needed to know to be saved.

It is obvious that the teaching of the Gnostics was diametrically opposed to apostolic teaching. What was needed therefore to combat this perversion of Christian truth was a summary of the Christian faith, an authoritative answer to the Gnostic threat. Consequently, summaries of apostolic Christianity began to emerge independently of one another in various parts of the Roman Empire. The similarity of content among these statements which came to be known as "rules of faith" is remarkable. Here is the rule of faith written by Irenaeus about A.D. 190:

> The Church, though dispersed throughout the whole world, even to the ends of the earth, has received from the apostles and their disciples this faith: (She believes) in one God, the Father Almighty, Maker of heaven, and earth, and the sea, and all things that are in them; and in one Christ Jesus, the Son of God, who became incarnate for our salvation; and in the Holy Spirit, who proclaimed through the prophets the dispensations of God, and the advents, and the birth from a virgin, and the passion, and the resurrection from the dead, and the ascension into heaven in the flesh of the beloved Christ Jesus, our Lord, and His (future) manifestation from heaven in the glory of the Father "to gather all things in one," and to raise up anew all flesh of the whole human race, in order that to Christ Jesus, our Lord, and God, and Saviour, and King, according to the will of the invisible Father, "every knee should bow, of things in heaven, and things in earth, and things under the earth, and that every tongue should confess" to Him, and that He should execute just judgment towards all; that He may send "spiritual wickednesses," and the angels who transgressed and became apostates, together with the ungodly, and unrighteous, and wicked and profane among men, into everlasting fire; but may, in the exercise of His grace, confer immortality on the righteous, and holy, and those who have kept His commandments, and have persevered in His love, some from the beginning (of their Christian course), and others from the date of their repentance, and may surround them with everlasting glory.[14]

The issue that the Gnostics had raised by their teachings was simply this: What is the substance of Christian teachings? And the second-century church responded with a resounding affirmation of the faith that came from the apostles. The following brief comparison of Gnostic teaching with apostolic teaching clearly shows that the second-century church rejected the false teaching of Gnosticism by asserting a summary of apostolic Christianity.

	Gnostic	*Christian*
God:	Dualism (two gods)	One: Father, Son, Holy Spirit
Authority:	Secret tradition	Tradition passed down from the apostles and their disciples; Holy Spirit through prophets
Creation:	An evil god made matter. Thus matter is evil.	The Father, the Almighty, who made the heavens and the earth
Jesus Christ:	An appearance, Jesus could not partake of flesh because flesh is matter and matter is evil. Known as Docetism (to seem); a great teacher.	Son of God Made flesh Born of a virgin Suffered Resurrected Ascended Will come again
Eschatology:	Absorption into divine. No resurrection of the flesh	To restore all things Raise up all flesh Judgment
Salvation:	Knowledge	By God's grace Life incorruptible a gift

It is important to recognize that the existence of these rules of faith represents a strong case to the effect that the substance of the church's belief and teaching was widely understood in the second century. Irenaeus did not pull his doctrine out of the air or create a counter-doctrine to the Gnostic point of view. He himself stated that his doctrine was no novelty, that it was, in fact, widely known, received, and confessed throughout the church universal:

> As I have already observed, the Church, having received this preaching and this faith, although scattered throughout the whole world, yet, as if occupying but one house, carefully preserves it. She also believes these points (of doctrine) just as if she had but one soul, and one and the same heart, and she proclaims them, and teaches them, and hands them down, with perfect harmony, as if she possessed only one mouth. For, although the languages of the world are dissimilar, yet the import of the tradition is one and the same.[15]

In summary then, by the end of the second century the church had an *authoritative source* and an *authoritative substance* of what she believed and taught. The authoritative source was the apostles. They had received their message from Christ and passed it on in the church. Both the oral and written traditions of the apostles, which they had transmitted to the church and which the church had received and guarded and passed on, were authoritative. In this sense, the Scriptures, both the Old Testament and what had been by that time recognized by the church (the four Gospels and the Pauline epistles), were the authoritative source that had been handed down by the apostles.

But the early church also recognized an authoritative substance within the authoritative source. This substance was a summary of the facts of faith, what came to be known as "the rule of faith." This rule, which appeared in various geographical areas of the Roman empire independently of one another, was regarded as a key to the interpretation of Scripture. Tertullian and Irenaeus both contended that the Scriptures, the authoritative source, could not be interpreted apart from the rule, the authoritative substance. It was the key to understanding the message of the apostles, handed down in their writings to the church, the keeper and guardian of the truth.

The Renewing Church Today

One of the major characteristics of the renewing church today is its concern for the unity of the church. This is not, as I have mentioned, a desire for organizational unity as such. Rather, the people of the renewing church are recognizing a grass roots unity of the people of God around the world and throughout history based on belief and experience.

The unity of experience is found in the saving reality of Jesus Christ. The unity of belief is found in Scripture as the source of truth and in the common creeds as the substance of truth. The creeds, such as the rule of faith and its more highly developed successors, the Apostles' Creed and the Nicene Creed, are looked upon as summaries of basic Christianity, summaries of faith around which every Christian group can gather.

For this reason the catechetical instruction of renewing churches is an explication of the Apostles' Creed (confirmed at baptism) and the Nicene Creed (proclaimed in worship). These creeds speak to the common confession of the churches of Christ throughout history and around the world. They are marks of a unity that already exists.

However, creeds are subject to interpretation, as is the Scripture. The problem of interpretation posed a formidable problem for the early church as it does for the church today. We turn now to the problem of interpretation in the early church to seek direction for the problem of interpretation in today's renewing churches.

15
THE QUEST FOR AN AUTHORITATIVE INTERPRETATION

If we were to ask a Christian of the first century, "What is your theology?" the answer would probably be little more than a bewildered stare. It would be much more appropriate to ask, "What do you believe?" or "What is your doctrine?" Doctrine, which is the word for Christian teaching, was closely associated with several other terms familiar to the early Christian: *kerygma, catechesis,* and *didascalia. Kerygma* points to the essential message that Christ died and was raised from the dead (Rom. 8:34) and to the manner in which this message was announced (preaching); *catechesis* refers to the oral teachings about Jesus, especially to the basic facts of the faith which the New Testament writers called the "milk" of the Word (Heb. 5:12–14; 1 Cor. 3:1–3); and *didascalia* embodies the doctrinal content of the Christian faith as it came to be understood and affirmed in the church, the meatier and heavier matters of the faith that the writer of Hebrews called "solid food" (5:14).

The point is that the early Christian was more familiar with terms such as *belief, doctrine,* and *confession* than with the term *theology.* Theology comes from the Greek word *theologia* and means *study of God.* But it was not used by the church as a technical term until the eleventh century when Abelard used it to apply to the whole of Christian teaching. However, it was primarily Thomas Aquinas in the thirteenth century who worked out a theory of theology as a science of revealed truths. Ever since Aquinas, the term has been used to refer to the analysis, application, and presentation of Christian beliefs, doctrines, and confessions.

Today we can use the word *theology* in an inclusive or exclusive way. If we talk about the theology of Christianity we refer to *all* the theologies or attempts to explain Christian truth. On the other hand we can use the term in an exclusive manner and speak of the theology of Calvin or Luther, Arminius, or our local pastor. Therefore, as we approach the subject which has come to be known as theology, we must separate what the church believes, teaches, and confesses from the human systems of theology which persons have developed. The fact that these can be two very different things, and that contemporary Christians sometimes confuse their personal theology with what the church has always taught, underscores the necessity to recover the historic theology of the church.

To begin with we need to make a distinction between "faith" and "formulation."

The word *faith* is not being used here in the sense of subjective response such as truth *(fiducia)* or relationship *(fides)*. Instead it is being used in the sense of the propositions of faith, the corpus of Christian doctrine, the convictions that are a necessary part of the Christian view of things *(credentia)*. Paul referred to this body of doctrine as the "gospel," the "pattern of sound words," the "truth" (2 Tim. 1:11–18). This is the truth taught by Jesus, transmitted by the apostles, and received in the church—truth that is basic and apostolic. While there are summaries of the truth in the New Testament, such as the sermons in

Acts, Paul's creedal statement in 1 Corinthians 15:3–5, and the confessional hymn of Philippians 2:1–11, the full-orbed truth became more specifically organized in the church in the second century. The word *faith* then is being used here in the specific sense of the *content* of Christianity as contained in "the rule of faith," the Nicene Creed, and the Apostles' Creed.

The word *formulation* is being used in the sense of theological thinking that goes beyond a mere affirmation of the faith, that is, human thinking about the truth. The fact of historical theology is that Christians throughout history have, in their thinking about the faith, attempted to organize their thinking into various categories of thought and to explain theological relationships between the parts of the whole to show their systematic unity. A glance at the history of theological formulations suggests that the articulation of theological systems is unavoidable. One only has to think of the outstanding systems of thought produced by the Cappadocian Fathers (Eastern Orthodox), Augustine, Aquinas, Luther, Calvin, and Arminius, to say nothing of the systems of thought propounded by theologians of lesser rank or movements such as Puritanism, Pietism, or Revivalism.

MAKING THE DISTINCTION BETWEEN FAITH AND FORMULATION

The problem among many Christians is that when the distinction between faith and formulation is not made, there is a tendency to identify the peculiarities of a particular formulation as *the* truth. For example, the Calvinists stress one system, the Arminians another, some try to bring the two together, and others stress no system at all. The fact is that beneath all these divisions there is a fundamental agreement. All evangelicals agree on the content of the gospel as defined by the early creeds. But not all evangelicals agree on the interpretation (formulation) of the facts of the faith.

The tragic result of our inability to separate formulation from faith and accept these differences is something like a theological legalism. Theological legalism is the insistence on a particular way of interpreting and organizing biblical data as the correct way of describing faith. Theologian Donald Bloesch calls this orthodoxism a tendency to view faith as assent to a particular dogma.

Theological legalism is often built around the differences of strong personalities or clear thinkers who by the magnitude of their ministry have created a following. This appears to be a basic reason for the existence of so many Christian subculture groups. Groups of people have fixed their leaders' theological insights into patterns of truth. Agreement with the leaders or founder, or in some cases with the interpretations given to the founder's insights, becomes a criterion for fellowship and ministry. Agreement with the teachings of Luther, Calvin, Menno Simons, Arminius, or Wesley marks a person as belonging to one group and not the other.

Because correct belief is often associated with a person or that person's system, adherence to the system is sometimes maintained by means of a party spirit. Unfortunately, when a subculture clings to the letter of its own formulation, it stands in danger of minimizing the primary essence of the Christian faith through its preoccupation with the preservation of its own secondary concerns.

Although theological legalism grows out of a sincere desire to do right, to think correctly, to apply Scripture to life, and to please God, it can become an inflexible tradition characterized by a spirit of exclusivism and division, with an inflexible self-righteousness, judgmental spirit, arrogance, and lovelessness.

The origins of the legalistic theology lie in a legalistic

methodology. Although all evangelicals accent the Bible as the final authority for faith and practice, there is much diversity among the subcultural groups on exactly how the authoritative Word is to be interpreted. It is not the diversity of interpretation that produces a methodological legalism, but the attitude that a particular subcultural interpretation is the only one that is right.

John Newport in *Why Christians Fight over the Bible* described the problem succinctly: "Many denominational and confessional groups appear to feel that the view of the Bible and the interpretations expressed by their founders or early leaders are to be exalted (and in some cases deified)."[16] This attitude becomes particularly suspect when one considers the various approaches to biblical interpretation among evangelicals: the Lutheran emphasis on justification as the key to interpretation; the Reformed covenantal approach; dispensationalism; literal *versus* spiritual interpretations of certain Old Testament prophecies; strict literalism *versus* openness to interpretation according to literary genre; and grammatical, historical, theological methods *versus* certain types of devotional and subjective interpretations.

Methodological legalism occurs when a subculture treats its hermeneutical system as the one correct approach, excluding (at least in part) the other schools, without taking into consideration the fact that their own school of interpretation is one among many. This closedmindedness is what theologian E. J. Carnell once referred to as the "cultic mind." The variety that is found in the Bible itself is bound to produce a broad spectrum of emphases. Unfortunately, these variables allow for conditions where "differences in interpretation interrupt the unity of the Spirit." Thus, Bernard Ramm has argued: "It is well for conservative Protestantism to discover bases of fellowship rather than of divergence, for a hermeneutical victory at the expense of Christian graciousness is hardly worth winning."[17]

While there are signs that this legalistic authoritarianism is cracking, its permeating presence restrains the winds of change and threatens to strangle the new spirit of a truly biblical and historic Christianity struggling to emerge in various stages of most evangelical subcultures.

We turn now to see how the terms *faith* and *formulation* and the idea of the difference between the two developed in the early church.

FAITH AND FORMULATION IN THE EARLY CHURCH

When we move into the third century and beyond, the distinction between the faith of the church and the theological formulation of the church becomes more clear. In the third century the task of *theoretical thinking* became increasingly important to the church. Between A.D. 300 and 600 the church was engaged in the task of formulating an explanation of what she already believed. This is evident in the Trinitarian, christological, and soteriological debates which dominated the third, fourth, and fifth centuries. (I do not deny formulation before the third century. Speaking in broad terms, the church at large began her formulation in the creedal controversies.)

An examination of these doctrinal controversies leads me to three observations:

First, the church always formulated her theology in conformity to the apostolic tradition. For example, Irenaeus's rule expressed faith in "one God . . . the Father Almighty; one Christ Jesus, the Son of God; and in the Holy Spirit." In similar fashion the rule speaks of the full humanity and divinity of the Son—"The Son of God who was made flesh." And it refers to the sinful state of man "in the godless and wicked and lawless and blasphemers among men," as well as to the fact that the incarnation, death, and resurrection of Jesus were "for our salvation." The issue of the trinitarian, christological, and soteriological controversies revolved around the *explanation* of these statements of faith. In other words, the church was engaged in a reflective exercise. She was thinking about the truths, which the church had always accepted, as *given* by God, *transmitted* by the apostles, and *received* by the church.

The second observation is that the church always thought about her faith within the context of her culture. For example, these controversies must be understood within the background of cultural, geographical, or philosophical differences. Both the trinitarian and the christological controversies were, at their center, exercises in communicating biblical truth into a Hellenistic frame of reference. The genius of both the Nicene Creed and the Chalcedonian definition is that the Fathers recognized the inadequacy of human language to capture the mystery of God as one yet three and the mystery of Jesus as fully human and fully divine.

The Fathers rejected the dualistic notions that tended to separate the Son from the Father and the human from the divine and affirmed, within a culture that was dualistically inclined, the holistic faith of the church. In this way the church succeeded in remaining faithful to apostolic Christianity while communicating the faith in a cultural form different from that in which the truth had been originally received and understood.

The soteriological controversy, which has to do with the nature of man, of sin and grace, of election and free will, and of the means of receiving the benefits of the death of Christ, and which has resulted in a number of different formulations, has never been as successful in uniting the church as the Nicene Creed and the Chalcedonian definition. While the Nicene Creed has gained universal acceptance and the Chalcedonian definition was accepted by all except the Monophysites, the same cannot be said for the formulations concerning man and salvation.

Although the entire church is united in its belief that man is a sinner and that Jesus Christ's death and resurrection procure salvation, there exists a number of explanations about man's sinful nature, and the means of receiving the benefits of Christ's death. The diversity on the soteriological question accounts for much of the diversity in the church. An examination of these differences can be accounted for, through the variety of influences that have given them shape—both cultural and philosophical. In other words, the church is not divided over whether man is a sinner whose only hope is in the death and resurrection of Christ, but in her disagreement on *how* this is to be explained.

A third observation is that the existence of disagreement forces the church to face the issue of private judgment. How can we determine which of the many interpretations we should follow? If there are many explanations, many theologies, many formulations, is the church left in a sea of relativity or is there a criterion by which these various interpretations may be judged? The answer to this question was provided by Vincent of Lérins (d. 450) in his *Commonitory:*

> I have often then inquired earnestly and attentively of very many men eminent for sanctity and learning, how and by what sure and so to speak Universal rule I may be able to distinguish the truth of Catholic faith from the falsehood of heretical pravity; and I have always, and in almost every instance, received an answer to this effect: That whether I or any one else should wish to detect the frauds and avoid the snares of heretics as they rise, and to continue sound and complete in the Catholic faith, we

must, the Lord helping, fortify our own belief in two ways: first, by the authority of the Divine Law and then, by the Tradition of the Catholic Church.

But here some one perhaps will ask, Since the canon of Scripture is complete, and sufficient of itself, what need is there to join with it the authority of the Church's interpretation? For this reason,—because, owing to the depth of Holy Scripture, all do not accept it in one and the same sense, but one understands its words in one way, another in another; so that it seems to be capable of as many interpretations as there are interpreters. For Novatian expounds it one way, Sabellius another, Donatus another, Arius, Eunomius, Macedonius, another, Plotinus, Apollinaris, Priscillian, another, Iovinian, Pelagius, Celestius, another, lastly, Nestorius another. Therefore, it is very necessary, on account of so great intricacies of such various error, that the rule for the right understanding of the prophets and apostles should be framed in accordance with the standard of Ecclesiastical and Catholic interpretation.

Moreover, in the Catholic Church itself, all possible care must be taken, that we hold that faith which has been believed everywhere, always, by all. For that is truly and in the strictest sense "Catholic," which, as the name itself and the reason of the thing declare, comprehends all universally. This rule we shall observe if we follow universality, antiquity, consent. We shall follow universality if we confess that one faith to be true which the whole Church throughout the world confesses; antiquity, if we in no wise depart from those interpretations which it is manifest were notoriously held by our holy ancestors and fathers; consent, in like manner, if in antiquity itself we adhere to the consentient definitions and determinations of all, or at least of almost all priests and doctors.[18]

Vincent of Lérins wrote from a high view of the church. For him, the church was not a mere human organization of people who believe, but the body of Christ inseparably united with the Holy Spirit. Thus, the Holy Spirit who is truly within the church brings consensus.

Although the suggestion of Vincent does not represent a doctrine as such, it does offer a helpful way to look at much of the theological diversity within the church. In essence it suggests that the church in the fifth century was united in its affirmation of the biblical framework of thought, but sought to sort out the thinking about this framework for determining which theology stood in the tradition of the apostles.

This brief summary suggests that the content of the Christian faith is basic to and even prior to theological formulation. The content of the church, which is based on the apostolic preaching and writings, is common to the whole church, belonging to the simple believer, to the theologian, the philosopher, or any other Christian thinker. It is the basic framework of truth from which all Christians live and think.

Theology, on the other hand, attempts to speak the faith through various cultural or philosophic forms in such a way that the biblical framework of truth is not violated. But the guide to Christian thinking, even here, the means by which Christians hold their subjective interpretations in check, is the rule of universality, antiquity, and consensus.

THE RENEWING CHURCH TODAY

Now the question is: How does this relate to the renewing church and to its recognition that there is only one church?

If we regard the summary of faith as the truth inherited from the apostles, then we need to recognize that beyond these statements there exist many theological explanations, most of which have not had the universal consent of the church. For example, in the sixteenth century there was a baffling array of confessional statements: Lutheran, Reformed, Anabaptist, and Catholic. These confessions are distinct from the creeds in that they are *more than* summaries of belief; they are *interpretations* of belief. Each confession constitutes a carefully designed interpretation of how the faith of the church is to be understood, yet each interpretation is based on the universally accepted creeds of the early church.

This variety of interpretations raises the question of how we are to deal with the differences among us. Some will argue that one confession is true and the others are false. This is certainly a possible answer, but as we have noted above, such an assertion runs the risk of posing two sources of truth—the Bible and a particular interpretation of it. Others will insist that no confession is to be regarded as true, and will reject all statements of faith including the creeds in favor of biblicism. This view runs the risk of failing to deal with the cults which also insist their views are derived solely from an inspired and inerrant Bible. A third approach is to conclude that all theologies result from thinking about truth. This view recognizes the difference between faith and formulation, yet regards formulation as a necessary task of the church.

Two arguments support this latter position. In the first place, interpretation of truth is based on human thinking. Confessions and books on systematic theology are the results of human thinking, not divine revelation. The limitations of the human mind are part of redeemed humanity so that, like Paul, all Christian thinkers, no matter how perceptive or scholarly, see "through a glass darkly."

Therefore, the tendency of human thinkers is to overemphasize some aspect of truth and interpret everything else in relation to it. Luther, for example, developed his entire theology around justification by faith; Calvin around the sovereignty of God; and Menno Simons around the theme of discipleship. No one human or group of humans is able to overcome the limitations fully enough to write a comprehensive, all-embracing theology.

Second, all interpretations of the truth must be understood in context. For example, the confessions of Luther and Calvin are understood best against the background of the late medieval interpretations of Christianity, which they regarded as perverse. In that context, as they broke from the Roman church, they accented the Word so strongly that a weakened view of the church, ministry, and sacraments resulted. What they did, although a "tragic necessity," as Jaroslav Pelikan describes it, was indeed a necessary corrective for that time and place. Nevertheless, it set into motion divisions and differences in the church which to this day have not been healed.

The interpretation of truth therefore is the ongoing activity of the church. The church is always at work formulating her faith in such a way that it remains faithful to its origins, yet communicates the truth within its own generation, geographical place, and cultural condition.

There are several important implications that proceed from recognizing the difference between faith and formulation. The first is that formulation does no violence to the essential truth of Christianity so long as the church accepts the historic substance of Christianity as the truth. In the case of a modern theological formulation, where the historic faith is regarded as untenable but the language of faith is retained, the formulation cannot be said to stand in continuity with the truth, for it denies the historic deposit, the apostolic testimony to the content of truth. However, where there is an honest acceptance of the historic contents of the faith, the thinking church is responsible to investigate the sources or attempt to articulate the faith within the context of a modern system of thought. But this thinking must always be brought under the judgment of the Scriptures and the testimony of history.

Second, however, the freedom to formulate human thinking about truth raises a certain cautionary note about the so-called doctrine of the private judgment of Scripture. Peter Toon in *The Right of Private Judgment* pointed out that the careless subjective approach to Scripture, which is a denial of the doctrine in its Reformational sense, "has been abused in much contemporary Evangelicalism" in that "little concern seems to be shown for setting the right context in which the Bible is to be understood and interpreted."[19] He has rightly argued that in the New Testament those who became converted were "expected to submit to the teaching of Christ and his Apostles"; that in fact private judgment really meant "making sure that one held firmly to the genuine Apostolic tradition."[20]

For this reason it is important for Christians to make sure that their ideas are tested by Scripture and the history of interpretation in the church. With so many subjective and ill-informed opinions filling the air, especially those coming from our current obsession with group discussions and sharing sessions, it is a good idea to test our insights by asking, "What has the church said?" This is a surer and safer test for truth than the personal insights that are being passed around in gatherings of well-intentioned believers.

A third implication that proceeds from the difference between faith and formulation is that it would be well for all of us to hold our theological formulations with a degree of tentativeness. This in no way means we are to be tentative about the gospel or the deposit of faith. The truth which has been revealed and passed down in history is unchangeable. Our conviction about it, our adherence to it, our propagation of it, is to be executed with firm assurance that it is true. But our formulation of that truth into a system, whether it be Calvinism, Arminianism, Dispensationalism, or whatever, must be expressed with tentativeness, even hesitancy.

We must learn to say, "it seems to me" or "my interpretation of Scripture seems to suggest" or "our church follows the interpretation of so-and-so who saw it this way." Here in the area of formulation we must learn to be *inclusive*, not exclusive. Obviously, such an approach serves the gospel, for it accents what we are sure about and makes what has been passed down in history unmistakably clear. It avoids making nonessentials essential and sets forth an attitude of Christian humility and graciousness that makes us accepting of and open to other Christians who also stand in the historic faith, but who articulate it through a different frame of reference.

A fourth implication is that thinking about the truth is the ongoing task of the church. To think about the truth and to articulate it in human form is consistent with the Incarnation. Mere biblicism is a denial of the human container through which truth is always known. The task of the church is to articulate truth within the context of history and culture. Such a task demands the critical use of human methods of thought—be they philosophical, psychological, anthropological, economic, or whatever. We need to learn to communicate truth in human garb in such a way that truth is not lost.

COMMUNICATING TRUTH IN HUMAN GARB

As the church faces the task of doing theology, the inevitable problem is that of communicating truth in human garb without accommodating truth to the garb through which it is being explained.

Because we interpret our faith through the glasses of

the culture in which we find ourselves, we tend then to impose cultural categories of thought on the faith, articulate our faith through these categories, and create an expression of Christianity peculiar to those cultural forms. Consequently, the faith becomes inextricably interwoven with a particular view of life or method. Our orthodoxy becomes not only believing the faith but also believing it within the life-view or by the method through which it has been expressed; the "grid" through which we are seeing theologically becomes a matter of belief just as much as the faith itself.

Helmut Thielicke addressed this problem in his work *The Evangelical Faith* by making a distinction between a theology of *actualization* and a theology of *accommodation*. A theology of actualization "always consists in a new interpretation of truth . . . the truth remains intact. It means that the hearer is summoned and called 'under the truth' in his own name and situation." On the other hand a theology of accommodation takes a different approach. It calls truth "under me" and lets me be its noun. It is pragmatic to the extent that it "assigns truth the function of being the means whereby *I master* life."[21] (Italics mine.)

Thielicke named accommodation theology the "cartesian" approach after René Descartes, the seventeenth-century philosopher who insisted that the starting point for truth was man: "I think, therefore I am." According to Thielicke there are, broadly speaking, two approaches in which Cartesian theology may be expressed—rationalism and experientialism. The reason these two approaches can be regarded as accommodation theologies is that "the receiving I is primary."[22] We might paraphrase it like this: "The Christian faith is a perfectly rational system about life. When *you* accept it and live by it *you* will really have life by the tail. *You* will be able to stand up strong and really face life"; or "What *you* need is an experience of Jesus

Christ. When *you* let him come into *your* life and take over, *you* will feel much better. Everything will fall in place for *you* and life will be beautiful." The emphasis is on the person, what the person does, how much better it is for the person, how much more in control of life the person will be.

On the other hand, actualization theology comes at a person's lost situation in an entirely different way. Because the person is "under the truth," an appeal is not made to the effect that the message of Christianity is "good for you." Instead, the truth is spoken in such a way that the person stands under the judgment of God, condemned because of sin, and under the sure wrath of God. Truth is proclaimed, not merely explained.

Through this proclamation the person is confronted then by truth—the truth about the human situation, the truth about personal involvement and participation in that situation, and the truth about the way Jesus Christ has met that situation and overcome it by his death and resurrection. Such an approach is a return to the kerygmatic preaching of the apostles.

The theology of actualization is the historic approach to communicating the gospel. The emphasis is on the biblical proclamation as truth and not the explanation that is often reliant on current philosophical categories of thought as well as subject to creaturely limitations. Final truth, it says, is always deeper and much more complex, more mysterious, than the best explanations we can offer.

This was the task of the church in the creedal era. How could it take the biblical concepts and articulate them within the framework of a Hellenistic mind-set, a Platonic or Neo-Platonic philosophy? For example, the trinitarian controversy employed Greek words like *homoousion* and *hypostasis* to communicate the unity and diversity of the Godhead. The christological controversy, as well, was settled through the use of Greek language and Hellenistic thought forms.

However, the genius of the creedal formulations is that *they did not elevate the methodology or the final theological form as truth in and of itself. Instead, the Nicene and Chalcedonian creeds pointed to the truth contained in Scriptures and summarized in the rule of faith as ultimately beyond the possibility of being captured in a comprehensive form.* In other words, the creeds wrote a negative theology: Jesus is not a creature as Arius taught; Jesus' humanity is not lost into divinity as Apollinarius taught, nor is his divinity a mere appendage to his humanity as some alleged Nestorius taught.

No, instead of allowing Jesus Christ to be defined as some wanted, the creeds affirmed the mystery of the unity of the Son with the Father and the completeness of full humanity and full divinity in the person of Jesus Christ. The creeds did not propagate a system, but affirmed the ultimate mystery of Christ through the thought patterns of the day. They "spoke" the biblical framework through a language and thought form different from the biblical language and thought forms without accommodating the truth to those forms.

The use of cultural forms as channels for truth has always been an issue in Christianity. In the early church much of theology was done through a Platonic grid. Aquinas expressed the Christian faith through the Aristotelian system of philosophy. Today we are in the process of developing an African theology and an Asian theology. These are simply a few examples of systems through which thinkers have attempted to communicate the Christian message. The problem we face is that when the method and the results of the method are made authoritative, Christ and the Christian message become blurred in the system.

The theology of the early church was able to deal with

the ambiguities of the Christian revelation. It didn't try to explain everything through a system. Instead, it developed creeds and theologies as *means* to communicate truth, not as *ends* in themselves. Hopefully, as we learn to articulate an actualization theology we will become not only more tolerant of people we disagree with but also more able to see the complexity of doing theological study, resulting in a reduction of our arrogance and pride as well as a growth in humility.

Such an attitude would free us to do theology within the framework of our own culture. We would begin to understand that the task of theology is not that of arriving at a fixed explanation which we forever freeze, but rather the calling to bring biblical thought to bear on ultimate questions in every culture and in every generation in such a way that it communicates the truth of apostolic Christianity to that situation.

Consequently, our systematic theology would forever become historical theology as the church would always be alive to the truth of Jesus Christ and the Word, not dead through a slavish allegiance to a system *about* the truth. This more biblical approach to theology will free us to make mistakes and to take the risk of thinking out loud—a risk that no one who is a slave to a system can take. Above all, this open-ended theology will free us to be related to Jesus Christ in a real way by allowing him and the truth about him in the Scriptures to be our final point of reference.

Conclusion

I began this section with a story about my dentist and his well-meaning assertion that he had as much truth as people who do biblical exegesis and theology. There is, of course, a certain degree of truth in his statement. What is important though, for him and other Christians like him, is to recognize that he has truth because it has been handed down from the apostles through the Scriptures and summarized by the creed. But my dentist and others like him need to be reminded that this is the common truth of the church, the truth that we all have received from the church which has handed it down to us.

Beyond this, the church has to face the difficult task of interpreting this truth in a particular time and place. And this is the task of the trained theologian, a task that goes beyond the ability of the average layperson.

What my dentist and other believing people have in common with the whole church is the Scriptures and the creed. This source and substance of Christian truth is held "everywhere, always and by all."

But the task of theology, which is the reflective and on-going task of the church, is usually done not by the dentists of the church, but by its theologians. And the theologian's work gets passed down to the people in the pew.

I sense that the renewing church is able to make this distinction so that what the church has always believed, everywhere and by all, is increasingly becoming the consensus of the renewing church. Greater authority is being given to the common tradition as less weight is placed on the theology of a particular tradition.

Therefore, in regard to authority, what we can expect in the renewing church is this: First, while the Bible will continue to be held in great authority, interest in debates about its authority will not be regarded as important, nor will the Bible be read and studied in search of a system of thought. Rather, the emphasis will fall on its teachings about the basic issues of faith and life. Renewing Christians are primarily interested in what the Bible has to say about daily living. They are concerned about improved relationships and what it means to follow Jesus.

Second, I think the creed will increasingly find its way into worship. It will be said (or sung) not as a mere intellectual statement of theological propositions. Rather, it will be looked upon as a witness to what is common to the whole church. Creeds such as the rule of faith, the Apostles' Creed, or the Nicene Creed will become increasingly important as symbols of Christian unity.

Third, in my opinion theology as a system of truth that distinguishes "us" from "them" makes little sense to renewalists. Theological systems will be studied from historical and sociological points of view. The emphasis will be upon the cultural factors that lie behind a particular system. This attitude will continuously free Christians from slavery to a particular system of thought. It will free them instead to emphasize the authority that lies behind the common tradition, the authority that brings the church together around the tapestry of Christ, church, worship, spirituality, and mission to the world.

In this way the New Testament literature, the creed, and theological reflection will function more as they did in the early church than they have in the more recent past. They will be viewed as a witness to the truth, placing Christ at the center with Scripture as the authoritative interpretation, with creed as an authoritative summary; and those points of theology having universal agreement in the church will be accepted as the common Christian tradition that unites all Christians everywhere.

*His essence indeed is incomprehensible,
so that his Majesty is not to be perceived
by the human senses; but on all his works he
hath inscribed his glory in characters so
clear, unequivocal, and striking, that the
most illiterate and stupid cannot exculpate
themselves by the pleas of ignorance.*

JOHN CALVIN

CONCLUSION

16
A MAJESTIC TAPESTRY

From time to time faculty members will take courses from their colleagues to learn something from a different field and integrate it into their own studies. Recently, a colleague of mine who teaches physics took a graduate course from me in which we were dealing with the Fathers of the early church.

During the course he kept calling attention to the fact that the concern to find a unifying principle in the field of Christian thought is exactly what is happening in science. (This is also true of all other areas of academic study.) He reminded us of the old Newtonian world-machine which treated things as if they stood alone. He emphasized how the old scientific view had influenced all areas of life and study. Nothing seemed to be interrelated. All of life looked like the alphabet lined up in a row with each letter independent of the other.

As I reflect on my own upbringing and my education in Christian schools, I am able to see how this view of the independence of all things affected my understanding of the Christian faith. Fifteen years ago I could not have explained how the work of Christ was related to the church, to worship, or the other areas discussed in this book.

However, a tremendous shift has taken place in the way we think about things in the last several decades. Specifically, that shift has been a move away from the independence of things to the interdependence of all things.

For example, my colleague explained more of what science is doing in its quest for a single unifying theory of everything. Scientists are looking for a link that ties together the four basic forces of nature—electromagnetism, gravity, the strong force, and the weak force. Currently, scientists think in terms of "superstrings" that bind together the four forces of nature. These superstrings are described as infinitesimally small, winding, curling one-dimensional strings that account for the unity of the four forces of nature and thus bring life together in a single whole.

This scientific quest for the unity of all things reminds me of the Pauline assertion that Christ is the one who unifies everything in himself. In Colossians 1 Paul tells us that Christ is the creator of all "things [that are] in heaven and that are on earth, visible and invisible" (1:16); that "in Him all things consist [hold together]" (1:17), and that "it pleased the Father that in Him all the fullness should dwell, and by Him to reconcile all things to Himself" (1:19–20). The unifying principle of all things is Christ.

I cannot comprehend the meaning of this sweeping proclamation. But I do know this: The early church Fathers who sought to work out in a more comprehensive manner the meaning of Paul's teaching have guided me into a view of life and faith that is significantly different from my old view.

I am no longer an atomist. The things of faith do not stand alone nor do they stand still. The Fathers of the church have taken me back into a dynamic world-view, an understanding of the interrelationship of all things. The faith, which once looked like an alphabet with everything standing independently and in a row, now looks like a majestic tapestry.

In this book I have made several observations about this phenomenon—observations that I have not attempted to prove in a scientific or statistical way. For example, I have suggested that the shift in thought from a static view of the universe to a more dynamic view has affected the people of this country who are under forty in ways that most cannot articulate. In the religious realm it has made the old views of the faith that were like the alphabet suspect. Since all of life has shifted toward the dynamic, the demand is for a Christianity that meets these needs. The renewing church is the church in quest of a more dynamic faith, a faith that has shifted away from the old debates between Christian groups. Instead, the renewing church seeks unity, spirituality, worship, and involvement in the lives of other people.

My argument has been that the renewing church, that new expression of the emerging church, whether Catholic, Protestant, evangelical, or charismatic, is unconsciously expressing a Christianity that has a deep kinship with the faith of the early church. What I sense is that many contemporary Christians who have been affected by the cultural change toward a more integrated and dynamic view of life are in quest of a faith that corresponds with their experience in general. For this reason an increasing amount of dissatisfaction is being expressed over a rationalistic and divided Christianity.

In this situation there is a return to the Christian tradition. For here is a faith that, like a tapestry, weaves everything in and out of the main thread—the work of Christ. My own experience with this rediscovered tapestry is a renewed and enriched faith. And I have talked with countless others who have experienced the same sense of newness in commitment through the insights of the early Christian tradition. Here, I believe, is a faith for our time, a faith that finds in the ancient Christian tradition, a power to enrich the contemporary church.

NOTES

Introduction
1. Jarslov Pelikan, *The Vindication of Tradition* (New Haven: Yale University Press, 1985), p. 3.
2. Chuck Smith, "Where Are They Taking Us?" *Christian Life*, January 1986, p. 27.
3. Philip Jacob Spener, *Pia Desderia* (Philadelphia: Fortress Press, 1964), pp. 81–85.

Section One: The Tradition about the Work of Christ
1. Irenaeus *Against Heresies* II, 2, 19.

Section Two: The Tradition about the Church
1. J. D. Douglas, ed., *Let the Earth Hear His Voice* (Minneapolis: Worldwide Publications, 1975), p. 5, article 6.
2. Ray Stedman, *Body Life* (Glendale: Regal, 1972), p. 15.
3. Clement *The First Epistle of Clement* 56.
4. *The Teaching of the Twelve Apostles* 9.
5. Cyprian *On the Unity of the Church* 4.
6. Cyril *Catechetical Lectures* XVIII, 3.
7. Bela Vassady, *Christ's Church: Evangelical, Catholic & Reformed* (Grand Rapids: Eerdmans, 1965), p.19ff.

Section Three: The Tradition about Worship
1. Justin Martyr, *The First Apology of Justin* 66.
2. See C. W. Dugmore, *The Influence of the Synagogue on the Divine Office* (London: Oxford, 1944), pp. 11–25.
3. Ruth Messenger in a pamphlet "Christian Hymns of the First Three Centuries" (New York: The Hymn Society of America, 1942), p. 5.
4. W. O. E. Oesterley, *The Jewish Background of the Christian Liturgy* (Oxford: Clarendon Press, 1925), p. 90.
5. Alexander Schmemann, *Introduction to Liturgical Theology* (London: The Faith Press, 1966), p. 44.
6. Schmemann, *Liturgical Theology,* p. 47.
7. Burdon Scott Easton, ed., *The Apostolic Tradition of Hippolytus* (Hamden: Archon Books, 1962), pp. 33–36.
8. William D. Maxwell, *An Outline of Christian Worship* (London: Oxford University Press, 1936), p. 112.
9. Justin *Apology* 50.

10. Ralph Martin, *The Worship of God* (Grand Rapids: Eerdmans, 1982), p. 215.
11. Gregory Dix, *The Shape of the Liturgy* (London: Sacred Press, 1945), p. 305.

Section Four: The Tradition about Spirituality

1. J. D. Douglas, ed., *Let the Earth Hear His Voice* (Minneapolis: Worldwide Publications, 1975), p. 7, article 6.
2. Easton, *The Apostolic Tradition of Hippolytus*, p. 20.
3. John Meyendorff, *St. Gregory Palamas and Orthodox Spirituality* (St. Vladimirs Press, 1974), p. 14.
4. J. Rodman Williams, *The Era of the Spirit* (Plainfield: Logos, 1971), p. 10.
5. Jim Wallis, *Agenda for Biblical People* (New York: Harper & Row, 1976), p. IX.
6. Hippolytus *The Apostolic Tradition* IV, 36, 3.
7. Ibid., IV, 36, 4.
8. Ibid., IV, 36, 6.
9. Schmemann, *Liturgical Theology.*

Section Five: The Tradition about the Mission of the Church

1. R. B. Kuiper, *God-centered Evangelism* (Grand Rapids: Baker, 1961), p. 80.
2. John R. W. Stott, *Fundamentalism and Evangelism* (Grand Rapids: Eerdmans, 1959), p. 72.
3. Jim Wallis, *Agenda for Biblical People* (New York: Harper, 1976), p. 23. See also David Moberg, *The Great Reversal: Evangelism Versus Social Concern* (Philadelphia: Lippincott, 1972).
4. George Eldon Ladd, *The Gospel of the Kingdom* (Grand Rapids: Eerdmans, 1959), p. 22.
5. Michael Green, *Evangelism in the Early Church* (Grand Rapids: Eerdmans, 1970).
6. Easton, *The Apostolic Tradition*, p. 41–49.
7. See Bruce J. Nicholls, *Defending and Confirming the Gospel:* The Report of the 1975 Consultation of the Theological Commission of the World Evangelical Fellowship (New Delhi, India: WEF Commission, 1975), pp. 36, 47.
8. Quoted by George Hoffman in "The Social Responsibilities of Evangelization," *Let the Earth Hear His Voice,* J. D. Douglas, ed., (Minneapolis: Worldwide Publications, 1975), p. 698.
9. C. H. Dodd, *The Apostolic Preaching and Its Development* (New York: Harper, 1939), p. 8.
10. Green, *Evangelism in the Early Church*, p. 204.
11. Hippolytus *The Apostolic Tradition* II, 17.

12. Lewis Sherrill, *The Rise of Christian Education* (New York: Macmillan, 1944), p. 149.
13. Philip Carrington, *Primitive Catechism* (Cambridge: The University Press, 1940), p. 13.
14. Justin *Apology* 61.
15. Hippolytus *The Apostolic Tradition* II, 20.
16. G. R. Beasley-Murray, *Baptism in the New Testament* (Grand Rapids: Eerdmans, 1973), pp. 267–268.
17. Hippolytus *The Apostolic Tradition* II, 21.
18. Larry Richards, *A Theology of Christian Education* (Grand Rapids: Zondervan, 1975), p. 16.
19. *Epistle to Diognetus* 5, 6.

Section Six: The Tradition about Authority

1. *Against Heresies* I, XXVII, 1.
2. Epistle of Barnabas 5, 1.
3. Gerald F. Hawthorne, ed., "A New English Translation of Melito's Paschal Homily" in *Current Issues in Biblical and Patristic Interpretation* (Grand Rapids: Eerdmans, 1975), p. 147.
4. *Against Heresies* I, XXVII, 2.
5. Clement *The First Letter of Clement* XLII, 1, 2.
6. *Against Heresies* III, 4.
7. John Chrysostom *Colossians,* homily IX.
8. Green, *Evangelism in the Early Church,* pp. 60–71.
9. Ibid., p. 60.
10. Ibid., p. 71.
11. John R. W. Stott, *Guard the Gospel* (Downers Grove: Intervarsity Press, 1973), p. 43–44.
12. Ibid., p. 50–51.
13. Eusebius, *Ecclesiastical History* Book III, XXII.
14. *Against Heresies* I, X, 1.
15. Ibid., I, X, 2.
16. John Newport, *Why Christians Fight over the Bible* (Nashville: Thomas Nelson, 1974) p. 14.
17. Bernard Ramm, *Protestant Biblical Interpretation* (Grand Rapids: Baker, 1956), p. 267.
18. Vincent of Lérins, *A Commonitory* II.
19. Peter Toon, *The Right of Private Judgment* (Portland: Western Conservative Baptist Seminary, 1975), p. 6.
20. Ibid., p. 12.
21. Helmut Thielicke, *The Evangelical Faith* (Grand Rapids: Eerdmans, 1974), p. 27.
22. Ibid., p. 38.

FOR FURTHER READING

Introduction

Bettenson, Henry. *The Early Christian Fathers*. New York: Oxford University Press, 1956. Selected readings from the Fathers of the second and third centuries.

———. *The Later Christian Fathers*. London: Oxford University Press, 1970. Selected readings from the Fathers of the fourth and fifth centuries.

Hargrove, Barbara. *Religion for a Dislocated Generation*. Judson, 1981. A discussion of the current generation, the social forces that have shaped them, and the type of religion they will most likely be drawn toward.

Kelly, J. N. D. *Early Christian Doctrine*. New York: Harper & Row, 1978. Widely accepted interpretation of the development of Christian thought in the first six centuries.

Kydd, Ronald A. H. *Charismatic Gifts in the Early Church*. Peabody, Mass: Hendrickson, 1984. An exploration into the gifts of the Spirit during the first three centuries of the Christian church.

Pelikan, Jarslov. *The Vindication of Tradition*. New Haven: Yale University Press, 1984. Shows how all disciplines are returning to tradition. Special emphasis is given to the mood of the current church to recover the tradition of the early church.

Webber, Robert. *Evangelicals on the Canterbury Trail: Why Evangelicals Are Attracted to the Liturgical Tradition*. Waco, Tex.: Word, 1985. Describes why many of the younger generation of evangelicals are returning to the mainline church.

Section I

Aulen, Gustav. *Christus Victor*. New York: MacMillan, 1969. A classic contemporary work that argues for the validity of the *Christus Victor* interpretation. Presents Irenaeus, Luther, Calvin among others.

Berkhof, Hendrik. *Christ and the Powers*. Scottdale, Pa.: Herald Press, 1977. A classical biblical treatment of the powers of evil and Christ's victory over them.

McDonald, H. D. *The Atonement of the Death of Christ in Faith, Revelation and History*. Grand Rapids: Baker, 1985. Presents and interacts with all the interpretations of the Atonement in the history of the church.

Morris, Leon. *The Cross in the New Testament*. Grand Rapids: Eerdmans, 1980. Deals with the biblical authors' views of the work of Christ.

Owen, John. *The Death of Death*. London: The Banner of Truth Trust, 1963. A distinguished Puritan writer reflects on the Atonement.

Pelikan, Jarslov. *Jesus Through the Centuries: His Place in the History of Culture*. New Haven: Yale University Press, 1985. A commentary on the interaction between images of Jesus and the changing culture throughout the centuries.

Turner, H. E. W. *The Patristic Doctrine of Redemption*. London: Mowbray, 1952. Deals with the early church Fathers. Widely accepted text.

Wallace, Ronald. *The Atoning Death of Christ*. Westchester, Ill.: Crossway, 1981. Popular commentary on biblical, historical, and contemporary views of the Atonement.

Section II

Banks, Robert. *Paul's Idea of Community: The Early House Churches in Their Historical Setting*. Grand Rapids: Eerdmans, 1980. Development of the early Christian church containing thoughtful commentary on the biblical text.

Berkhouwer, G. C. *The Church*. Grand Rapids: Eerdmans,

1976. Excellent commentary on the marks of the church—One, Holy, Catholic, and Apostolic.

Dulles, Avery. *Models of the Church*. New York: Doubleday, 1974. Sets forth five models of the church which have emerged in the church through centuries—institutional, mystical, herald, servant, sacramental.

Hauerwas, Stanley. *A Community of Character*. Notre Dame: University of Notre Dame Press, 1981. Calls upon the church to become in Christ what it is called to be.

Jay, Eric G. *The Church: Its Changing Image Through Twenty Centuries*. Atlanta: John Knox Press, 1978. A survey of the church in various cultural situations throughout history.

Minear, Paul S. *Images of the Church in the New Testament*. Philadelphia: Westminster Press, 1960. Excellent development of the church as the people of God, the new creation, the fellowship in faith, and the body.

Snyder, Howard A. *A Kingdom Manifesto: Calling the Church to Live Under God's Reign*. Downers Grove, Ill.: InterVarsity Press, 1985. Emphasis on building the church as community under the lordship of Christ.

Willimon, William. *What's Right About the Church*. San Francisco: Harper & Row, 1985. Stresses the church as the incarnate body of Christ, an alternative society in the world.

Section III

Baptism, Eucharist and Ministry: Faith and Order Paper No. 111. Geneva, Switzerland: World Council of Churches, 1982. A statement of Christian unity based on the common tradition of the early church.

Martin, Ralph. *Worship in the Early Church*. Grand Rapids: Eerdmans, 1974. Emphasis on the biblical texts pertaining to worship.

Porter, H. Boone. *Keeping the Church Year*. New York: Seabury Press, 1977. Comments on the meaning of each season of the church year.

Preston, Geoffry. *Hallowing the Time: Meditations on the Cycle of the Christian Liturgy*. New York: Paulist Press, 1980. A personal prayer and devotional guide through the church year.

Saliers, Don E. *Worship and Spirituality*. Philadelphia: Westminster Press, 1984. Shows how to bring one's spirituality into the life of worship.

Searle, Mark, ed. *Liturgy and Social Justice*. Collegeville: The Liturgical Press, 1980. Shows how worship compels us to be involved in a concern for social justice.

Smolarski, Dennis C. *Eucharistia: A Study of the Eucharistic Prayer*. New York: Paulist Press, 1982. A detailed historical, theological, and contemporary study of the prayers said at the Table of the Lord.

Webber, Robert. *Worship Is a Verb*. Waco: Word, 1985. Sets forth four principles of worship rooted in the biblical and historical tradition of the church.

—————. *Worship Old and New*. Grand Rapids: Zondervan, 1982. Biblical, historical, and theological backgrounds to worship.

White, James F. *Introduction to Christian Worship*. Nashville: Abingdon, 1980. An introduction to the basic categories of Christian worship such as Word, sacrament, time, space.

Section IV

Bloom, Anthony. *Living Prayer*. Springfield: Templegate, 1966. Widely regarded as the most important book on prayer in print.

Bouyer, Louis. *Introduction to Spirituality*. Collegeville: Liturgical Press, 1961. A classic work introducing prayer, sacramental life, Christian asceticism, rhythms of spirituality, etc.

Bradshaw, Paul F. *Daily Prayer in the Early Church*. New York: Oxford University Press, 1982. Excellent insight into the development of prayer and its content in both Eastern and Western traditions of the early church.

Foster, Richard. *The Celebration of Discipline*. San Francisco: Harper & Row, 1978. Presents the inward, the outward, and the corporate disciplines of spirituality.

_____. *The Freedom of Simplicity*. San Francisco: Harper & Row, 1981. Discusses how our lives may become models of simplicity and the impact of such a choice on spirituality.

Job, Rueben R. and Norman Shawchuck. *A Guide to Prayer for Ministers and Other Servants*. Nashville: The Upper Room, 1983. A series of personal weekly prayer retreats organized around the theme and texts of the church year.

Meyendorff, John. *St. Gregory Palamas and Orthodox Spirituality*. Crestwood, N.Y.: St. Vladimir Seminary Press, 1974. Presents spiritual tradition of the monks of the East with particular emphasis on Hesychasm.

Schmemann, Alexander. *For the Life of the World*. Crestwood, N.Y.: St. Vladimir Seminary Press, 1973. Commentary on how the liturgy relates to all of life.

_____. *Great Lent*. Crestwood, N.Y.: St. Vladimir Seminary Press, 1973. Interprets Lent and shows how one may travel through that important time in a spiritual way.

Ware, Timothy. *The Orthodox Way*. Crestwood: St. Vladimir's Press, 1980. An introduction to the spirituality of the early church Fathers and what we can learn from them.

Webbe, Gale D. *The Shape of Growth*. Wiltron: Morehouse Barlow, 1985. Thoughtful biblical and historical comments on conversion, discipline, confession, prayer, and other subjects of spirituality.

Webber, Robert. *The Book of Family Prayer*. Nashville: Thomas Nelson, 1986. A table liturgy for the family organized around the church year. Also includes table liturgies for special occasions such as birthdays, etc.

Section V

Clarke, Thomas E. *Above Every Name*. New York: Paulist Press, 1980. Presents a case for the lordship of Christ over all social systems.

Cochrane, Charles Norris. *Christianity and Classical Culture*. The classical interpretation of the relationship between church and society in the first six centuries of the church.

Duggan, Robert. *Conversion and the Catechumenate*. New York: Paulist Press, 1984. Discusses conversion in the Bible and comments on the developmental understanding of the conversion process.

Dujanier, Michael. *The Rites of Christian Initiation*. New York: Sadlier, 1979. Historical and theological reflections in the catechumenate as an organizing principle for evangelism.

————. *A History of the Catechumenate*. New York: Sadlier, 1979. Presents the development of the catechumenate as a means of evangelism in the early church.

Neville, Gwen Kennedy and John H. Westerhoff, III. *Learning Through the Liturgy*. New York: Seabury Press, 1978. Emphasizes how worship and education bring the gospel and Christian formation together.

Rite of Christian Initiation of Adults: Provisional Text. Washington: United States Catholic Conference, 1974. Contains the liturgies for a liturgical evangelism in the local church.

Wallis, Jim. *The Call to Conversion: Recovering the Gospel for These Times*. San Francisco: Harper & Row, 1981. Emphasizes how evangelism and obedience are related. Stresses evangelism in worship and community.

Webber, Robert. *Celebrating our Faith: Evangelism Through Worship*. San Francisco: Harper & Row, 1986. Discusses the relevance of third-century evangelism through worship for today. Goes through the seven steps of evangelism and worship, showing biblical roots, historical example, and contemporary application.

_____. *The Church in the World: Opposition, Tension, Transformation*. Grand Rapids: Zondervan, 1986. Develops the relationship between church and world through history and suggests a model for our time.

Westerhoff, John H. *Values for Tomorrow's Children: An Alternative Future for Education in the Church*. Philadelphia: Pilgrim Press, 1970. Argues for an education that occurs through involvement in the life of the church—its worship, social concern, community, etc.

_____. *Inner Growth, Outerchange: An Educational Guide to Church Renewal*. New York: Seabury Press, 1979. Argues that the church does not need to choose between inner piety and outer social concern. Both are needed.

_____. *A Pilgrim People: Learning Through the Church Year*. New York: Seabury Press, 1984. Shows how each of the Christian seasons shapes our spiritual life and pilgrimage.

Section VI

Barbour, Ian. *Myths, Models and Paradigms*. New York: Harper & Row, 1974. An important book showing how religion and science are moving away from fixed systems of thought to affirm paradox and variety. Applied to theology.

Fackre, Gabriel. *The Christian Story: A Narrative Interpretation of Basic Christian Doctrine*. Grand Rapids: Eerdmans, 1984. Theology written out of the story of the living, dying, and rising to life of Christ.

Flannery, Austin P., ed. *Documents of Vatican II*. Grand Rapids: Eerdmans, 1975. These documents call for the restoration of the common tradition among Catholics.

Johnston, Robert. *The Use of the Bible in Theology: Evangelical Options*. Atlanta: John Knox, 1985. In this book ten evangelical theologians describe how they use the Bible in doing theology. The variety of approaches is an interesting commentary on both the unity and diversity among evangelicals.

Kelly, George A. *The New Biblical Theorists*. Ann Arbor: Servant Books, 1983. A Catholic assessment of modern biblical views with a call to restore the traditional view of the Bible.

Leith, John H. *Creeds of the Churches*. New York: Doubleday, 1963. Contains creeds of the various churches throughout history. Introduction provides an excellent introduction to creeds as witness to truth.

Pinnock, Clark. *The Scripture Principle*. San Francisco: Harper & Row, 1984. Discusses current issues in biblical authority and offers a middle-way solution.

Rodgers, Jack B. and Donald K. McKim. *The Authority and Interpretation of the Bible*. San Francisco: Harper & Row, 1979. Development of the doctrine of Scripture throughout history.

Wainwright, Geoffrey. *Doxology: The Praise of God in Worship, Doctrine, and Life*. New York: Oxford University Press, 1980. A systematic theology written out of the liturgy.